AF328703

ON THE ORIGINS OF JEWISH SELF-HATRED

ON THE ORIGINS OF
JEWISH SELF-HATRED

PAUL REITTER

PRINCETON UNIVERSITY PRESS
PRINCETON AND OXFORD

ON THE ORIGINS OF JEWISH SELF-HATRED

PAUL REITTER

PRINCETON UNIVERSITY PRESS
PRINCETON AND OXFORD

Copyright © 2012 by Princeton University Press

Published by Princeton University Press, 41 William Street,
Princeton, New Jersey 08540
In the United Kingdom: Princeton University Press, 6 Oxford Street,
Woodstock, Oxfordshire OX20 1TW

press.princeton.edu

All Rights Reserved
ISBN 978-0-691-11922-9

Library of Congress Control Number: 2012931223

British Library Cataloging-in-Publication Data is available

This book has been composed in Minion and Univers
Printed on acid-free paper ∞
Printed in the United States of America

10 9 8 7 6 5 4 3 2 1

CONTENTS

Introduction   1

Part One: Genealogical Imperatives   5

Part Two: The Birth of "Jewish Self-Hatred" and the
    Spirit of Interwar Europe   45

Part Three: Prominence: The Making of Theodor
    Lessing's Book *Jewish Self-Hatred*   75

Conclusion   121

Notes   127

Select Bibliography   155

Index   161

Acknowledgments   165

ON THE ORIGINS OF JEWISH SELF-HATRED

Terminology is the root of all unhappiness.
—ANTON KUH

Origins and original meanings cling to some concepts more than to others. Or so it can seem. Take "antisemitism," which entered the popular lexicon in 1879. It was then that a journalist in Germany dubbed his own outlook "antisemitic," because he wanted to mark the difference between himself and bigots he deemed less serious. The applications and connotations of the term soon expanded. Within a few years, orthodox Jews had started using it to characterize their reform rivals. But no matter: "antisemitism" has long been *the* key category in the study of anti-Jewish prejudice, and in a way, this history has freed the concept from its beginnings. Haven't we come to think that if a lot of us can work with "antisemitism" judiciously, then just about everyone should be able to? After all, when "antisemitism" is wielded as a means of inciting or smearing, we say little about the pull of old patterns. It is, for the most part, the wielder who gets the blame.

Now consider "Jewish self-hatred." We find it, too, relied upon at the highest levels of scholarship. Yet "Jewish self-hatred" hasn't established itself there to the same degree as "antisemitism," and this difference appears to have made, well, all the difference.[1] For when someone employs "Jewish self-hatred" reductively or vituperatively—in whatever context—it often happens that the phrase's history is held responsible, especially its early history. That "Jewish self-hatred" took shape as a polemical weapon, that it rose to prominence as an instrument of censure—these views have staple-like status in critical responses to the concept, quite a few of which feature claims about how the concept's original meanings have managed to hold their ground. Only "Jewish self-hatred" neither came about nor gained currency in the ways I've just described. And so a revision, if not an apologia, is in order.

This isn't to suggest that every attempt to write the genealogy of "Jewish self-hatred" has been carried out in the service of a critique. There are other accounts, accounts that don't seek, in effect, to discredit the concept. But these have proven to be almost as misleading as the most programmatic ones, which raises a series of questions, beginning with: why? Why has the emergence of "Jewish self-hatred" been so hard to track? What is it about the history of the concept, and what is it about how we practice conceptual history, that has made for such a high rate of failure? In part 1, I offer some answers. Doing so will involve examining the prehistory of "Jewish self-hatred," which is, as it happens, also important for understanding the genesis of that particular notion.

Indeed, one of the aims of this book is to show that "Jewish self-hatred" was forged in opposition to the terms that look like—and that have been seen as—its precursors.[2] Contrary to what scholars and critics often argue, "Jewish self-hatred" didn't come into being as a straightforward extension of a long-running, mostly censorious discussion of Jewish self-contempt. It was formulated, rather, to promote a very different way of thinking. For Anton Kuh and Theodor Lessing—the semisuccessful authors who, respectively, coined and popularized the concept—"Jewish self-hatred" was a heading that stood at once for a very big problem and its world-saving solution. In their works, "Jewish self-hatred" has, along with various other connotations, nothing less than redemptive meanings.[3]

Part 2 focuses on Kuh, part 3 on Lessing. Each tells the story of how its subject came to use "Jewish self-hatred" as he did. In both cases, we will hear about a host of factors. Both Kuh and Lessing had personal stakes in their conceptual endeavors, for example. They grew up in assimilated—or rather, assimilationist—German-Jewish homes, which is where their interest in the dynamics of assimilationism began. Furthermore, in defining "Jewish self-hatred," Kuh and Lessing deal mostly with their own ranks: German-Jewish intellectuals. Hence Alfred Döblin's assessment of the book in which, with plenty of shtick, Kuh unveils his term; upon reading *Jews and Germans* (1921), Döblin remarked, "What good is all the wit in the world if you're only talking about five acquaintances?"[4]

Of course, we could say the same thing about many reckonings with the Jewish Question. What caused Döblin to wonder about Kuh's approach is probably that Kuh relies on local reference points in discussing not simply the plight of the Jews, but also the fate of all humanity. In fact, "Jewish self-hatred" is, in a sense, a consequence of the First World War and the large-scale reorienting to which the war led. Kuh's belief that much had become clearer and much had changed helped prompt him to call for a terminological shift, his logic being that the new situation should have at least elements of its own vocabulary. Generally speaking, the war radicalized both Kuh's and Lessing's thought, while fostering, as well, greater complexity. Though hardly identical, both their responses to the events of 1914–18 entailed cultivating incongruous—and even incompatible—ideas about the ills of modern society. And as we will see, both Kuh and Lessing used "Jewish self-hatred" to resolve those tensions, and in such a way that the concept signifies just the capacity through which the Jews could teach the world how to heal itself.

Kuh found inspiration for his paradoxes in a number of sources. Some have faded from view as much as he has, as, for example, the psychologist Otto Gross. Others are as famous as ever. Foremost among the latter group is Nietzsche, who once spoke of "Jewish hatred" as "the profoundest and most sublime kind of hatred, previously unknown on earth and capable of creating ideals and reversing values."[5] Lessing, too, built upon Nietzsche's thought, and Lessing almost certainly drew on Kuh's *Jews and Germans* when he wrote his higher-profile book, *Jewish Self-Hatred* (1930). What, then, about the effect of that work? Did the affirmative meanings that Lessing gave to "Jewish self-hatred" ever stick well enough to make their presence felt? For reasons that should become clear, this question is a good point from which to begin a new genealogy of "Jewish self-hatred"—and thus it is also a good place to break off.

PART ONE

Genealogical Imperatives

The best author will be the one who
is ashamed of being a writer.
—FRIEDRICH NIETZSCHE

In the spring of 1931, Theodor Lessing set off from his home in Hanover to take his first and, as it would turn out, his only trip to the Middle East. The journey had been a long time in coming. A feminist, a socialist, and an anti-noise and anti-imperialism activist who earned his living mainly as a kind of philosophical feuilletonist, Lessing was, as well, a Zionist, and at the age of fifty-nine, he had been one for more than thirty years. To his delight, Lessing learned in Jerusalem that his work had preceded him there. A letter to his wife excitedly conveys the news: "Not far from the Wailing Wall, a Jew recognized me and addressed me by my name. He had just bought my 'Jewish self-hatred book'—all the bookstores in the city have it."[1]

If Lessing was glad to see his latest monograph being sold in Jerusalem, he hardly seemed surprised, and why should he have been? After all, *Jewish Self-Hatred* was an undertaking that important Zionists had backed. Siegmund Kaznelson, the director of the Jüdischer Verlag (or Jewish Press), had made Lessing's study part of the press's new "Zionist book league" series. Robert Weltsch, a leader of the Zionist movement in Germany, had encouraged Kaznelson in this. Not that he had needed nudging: both men, and especially Kaznelson, thought that *Jewish Self-Hatred* would serve the Zionist cause extraordinarily well. Upon reading selections, Kaznelson spoke of the book as being a "Zionist propaganda coup," and of how it would be "sensational in the extreme."[2] He predicted, moreover, that Lessing's work would "in its effects far surpass" whatever else he might opt to include in the "Zionist book league" venture.[3]

To say that he was right isn't saying much, since infighting at the press soon killed the series. But Kaznelson and Weltsch also came close to the mark about the impact of Lessing's volume. If the book failed to create a sensation, it succeeded in causing a stir, quickly popularizing the catchy young term in its title: a product of the early interwar years, the concept "Jewish self-hatred" wasn't yet a decade old. Furthermore, with its mix of pathos-laden homily, colorful theory, and concise biography, Lessing's text won over a parade of Zionist readers. Writing in *Self-Defense* in 1930, Felix Weltsch, a cousin of Robert, gave this gushing appraisal: "The well-known philosopher" has "brought forth a deep-reaching psychology of the Jewish spirit," which "shows us how to find the way that leads out of negation and decline, and to healing and freedom."[4] Kafka's friend Max Brod, whom Lessing had propitiated for years, would take the opportunity to flatter Lessing back, hailing *Jewish Self-Hatred* as a work of "genius."[5] According to an anonymous reviewer for *The Voice*, another Zionist newspaper, Lessing deftly illuminated the "tragedy of the Jew who tries to flee from himself and his Jewishness."[6] In the *Jüdische Rundschau*, perhaps the most respected organ of German Zionism, an unnamed author enthused over the "liberating force" of Lessing's words, as well as their ability to open up "new perspectives on a great Jewish future."[7] Meanwhile, a less mainstream Zionist publication thanked Lessing for revealing—"with uncommon acumen"—the "deep psychic abyss that is Jewish self-hatred."[8]

Anti-Zionists, on the other hand, tended to be harsh in their assessments, though they weren't the only ones to express scorn. Freud famously disliked Lessing's book, in which psychoanalysis figures as a consequence of Jewish self-hatred, but he stated his disdain curtly and informally.[9] It was the newspaper of the integration-minded Central Association of German Citizens of the Jewish Faith that felt compelled to carry out a thorough public reckoning. Its upshot wasn't so much that Jewish self-hatred didn't exist or warrant scrutiny, as that with their antirationalist bent, Lessing's ideas about Jews and Judaism were misguided to the point of making little sense. Lessing had hardly gone out of his way to head off such doubts. To the contrary, quite a few passages in *Jewish Self-Hatred* read like attempts to speak the effusive language of Jewish renewal that Gershom Scholem dubbed "Buberdeutsch," after the Zionist philosopher Martin Buber (and his rhetorical excesses). Lessing's book proclaims, for example, that Jewish self-hatred won't abate until there are Jews who spend their time "praying before the trees and the clouds."[10] Summing up his or her objections, the reviewer for the Central Association's newspaper dismisses such lines as absurdities. They have, according to the reviewer, nothing to offer the Jewish *Geist*, which should spend its time immersed in nothing other than *Geist*.[11]

In an essay published in *Morning*, a magazine with ties to the Central Association, the Leipzig-based rabbi Felix Goldmann strikes a more respectful tone, stressing at the outset that Lessing's writings haven't received as much praise as they deserve. Goldmann also gives Lessing credit for drawing attention to the blight of Jewish self-hatred, whose toll of torment, he maintains, hasn't been emphasized enough. But in the end, Goldmann develops a sharp critique of Lessing's text. It seemed to him that if Lessing's focus was well founded, the execution of his analysis had gone badly awry. Lessing had done nothing less, in fact, than lose sight of one of his own suggestions about what the concept "Jewish self-hatred" should be taken to mean. For while all of them were troubled, the six assimilated intellectuals whom Lessing offers as his case studies didn't all display, as Goldmann puts it, "the hatred the renegade harbors for the community he's turned his back on." Hence the verdict: "Lessing's examples don't support his theory."[12]

When we set up this reception as I have just done, namely, as a series of Zionist and anti-Zionist responses to an ardent, officially sanctioned Zionist work, outfitted with a fresh label for what its author treats as the given of Western Jewry's malaise, then the reception unfolds as we might expect it to. But if I had begun with an overview of more recent accounts of Lessing's book, and proceeded from there to survey the early debate about it, the tenor and the dimensions of the debate would be less self-evident. Indeed, they would likely come as a surprise. This isn't simply because over the past half-century Lessing's readers have been scholars, who have, naturally enough, transformed the meaning of his study by bringing to it their own questions, concepts, and interpretive strategies. Here the gap between early and later understandings also has to do with a tendency to misrepresent both the historical place of Lessing's signature usage and its explicit content, and the gap is therefore a problem, a problem that stems from a larger one. Despite our interest in how the notion "Jewish self-hatred" was born, we still don't have a persuasive genealogy of the term.

II

Why is that so? To begin with, "Jewish self-hatred" has a way of calling forth the kinds of polemical measures its critics decry, and this cycle has skewed inquiries into its past. Take the case of Allan Janik, the co-author of the widely read, well-received book *Wittgenstein's Vienna* (1973). Put off by how his fellow historians of ideas had worked with "Jewish self-hatred," Janik undertook to show "how thoroughly" the concept has been "tinged" with essentialism from the start, and how it has, as a result, led to bad exegesis.[13] Certainly Janik had grounds for suspicion when he wrote the essay "Viennese Culture and the Jewish-Self-Hatred Hypothesis" (1987). Among contemporary scholars, Janik charged no less a personage than Peter Gay with misusing the category "Jewish self-hatred," and he did so with some justification.

Gay, to be sure, had framed the issue of Jewish self-contempt in a variety of ways. He had suggested that even the most vicious Jewish self-skewering could be well intentioned. What sometimes drove it, according to Gay, was less an urge to make other Jews suffer than the sense that if other Jews would just shape up, antisemites would have nothing to inveigh against, or be violent about—self-hatred as tough love, however misguided.[14] Echoing W.E.B. Dubois and Isaiah Berlin, Gay had also put forth the point that self-directed bigotry among minorities is a natural, hard-to-avoid phenomenon, if not a desirable one.[15] In *Freud, Jews, and Other Germans* (1978), Gay observes, "For like all minorities, Jews too incorporated at least some of the prejudices and stereotypes of the dominant majority around them."[16] As if that sounded too vague and too abstract, Gay goes for concreteness and immediacy in his next sentence. He asks, "What Jew has not cringed at what he regards as the ostentatious behavior—loud voices, sharp clothing, flashing jewelry, sported by those who 'look Jewish' in a theatre lobby, a restaurant, a bus?" In addition to these normalizing sketches, Gay draws a thorough and far from unsympathetic portrait of his chief instance of Jewish self-hatred, the conductor Hermann Levi, who didn't so much feel ashamed of his fellow Jews, as subject himself to painful antisemitic razzing from Richard Wagner and his circle.[17]

But where he makes an example of Gay, Janik focuses on Gay's handling of a different historical actor: the fin-siècle philosopher Otto Weininger. As he introduces Levi's outlook, Gay, in effect, dismisses Weininger's brief life and occasionally bizarre thought as cautionary tales that do little more than illustrate the "terrifying power of *Selbsthaß*."[18] And while Gay himself is otherwise fairer, this move isn't a lonely aberration. Elsewhere, too, the concept "Jewish self-hatred" appears to have abetted in academic writing a not-so-scholarly rushing to judgment, with the judged most often being early twentieth-century German Jews whose rhetoric seems to mirror the antisemitic discourses of their day. Consider Jacques Le Rider's response to the Viennese firebrand Karl Kraus. Or more specifically, consider how in 1987, Le Rider, a leading theorist of Viennese modernism, dealt with a provocatively worded, yet also densely paradoxical essay by Kraus. In Le Rider's brusque determination, Kraus's "Heine and the Consequences" (1910) "can only really be understood as yet another symptom of *jüdischer Selbsthaß*."[19]

Thus Janik had a point when he told scholars to apply the notion "Jewish self-hatred" more circumspectly, or not at all. He also had one when he reminded readers that *Sex and Character* (1903), which young Weininger finished just before he shot himself, and which would become the world's best-selling revised Ph.D. thesis, has more complexity than its often-cited low moments imply. Pronouncements like "there has never been a noble man of Jewish blood" and "women at least have faith in men, the Jew believes in nothing" are, as Janik stressed, largely confined to a single chapter in Weininger's book.[20] But what finally matters for us is Janik's historical argument, and where Janik sets about trying to make it stick, he himself operates all too hastily. Beyond wrongly stating that Lessing "coined" the term "Jewish self-hatred," Janik hangs his whole theory of Lessing's fateful essentialism on an anachronistic interpretation of a misquotation.

Having repeatedly called Lessing's understanding of Jewish self-hatred "racist," and even characterized it as being "based upon a racism which is just as crude as anything the most vulgar Nazi ideologues might have asserted," Janik marshals a single line of text in support of his claims.[21] The line reads, "Weininger hated his blood, and his blood was Jewish blood."[22] Yet contrary to what Janik assumes, it was possible in Lessing's day to speak of "Jewish blood" without advancing Nazi-style racism. In the mouth of a Nazi, the phrase might have sent a chill down the spine. More often, however, "Jewish blood" still had "Jewish descent" as its primary meaning, as it did for, say, Walter Benjamin in 1931.[23] Furthermore, if Lessing was unusually provocative in ascribing a biological component to Jewish identity—he insisted that Jews are more "Aryan" than Germans—he was also uncommonly direct in challenging the extreme biological determinism of the Nazis, who had him murdered in 1933. And in the end, Lessing saw Jewishness as a distinctive constellation of attributes that shared values and experiences had produced, for the most part. So when, in *Jewish Self-Hatred*, Lessing repudiates "racist antisemitism" only to mention "Jewish blood," he isn't necessarily contradicting himself.[24]

Beyond all that, Lessing didn't actually write, "Weininger hated his blood." His phrasing, rather, is "Weininger hated blood," and the addition of the word "his" is no insignificant error.[25] Transforming "hated blood" into "hated his blood" distorts Lessing's message, all the more so because of what Janik does with the change. Indeed, Janik leans on precisely the recast wording in emphasizing how much Lessing's conception of Jewish self-hatred relies on "racism." The idea is that, for Lessing, the term "Jewish self-hatred" signifies "the hatred of *Jewish* blood by a person of Jewish blood." But by the remark that gets lost, Lessing is proposing something very different. When he wants Jews to pray before the trees and the clouds, Lessing is making the case that Jews have become unhealthily estranged from, and hostile to, the messy, bloody world outside their mental abstractions; and he is doing likewise when he notes (or imagines) that Weininger "hated blood." Issues such as this one make up the thematic nub of Lessing's book, much more than Weininger's disparagement of Jews and Judaism does. It was these preoccupations that frustrated Goldmann, the rabbi in Leipzig. He opened Lessing's study hoping to gain insight into the psychology of "renegade" Jews who detest their own heritage, and he felt let down when Lessing failed to oblige him.

What proposition in intellectual history could be more damning than the claim: this concept rests on racism as bad as that of the least-refined Nazis? Yet Janik's standing as the most draconian critic of the concept "Jewish self-hatred" didn't last long. His genealogy is, in fact, quite a bit milder than some of its more recent counterparts. So it appears that "Jewish self-hatred" has become an even stronger magnet for invective. The main reason for this development is hard to miss. As Arab-Israeli relations have worsened over the past decade, the term "Jewish self-hatred" has been thrust back into prominence. "Back," because during the "American-Jewish Cold War" of the 1950s and 1960s, "Jewish self-hatred" served as a popular cudgel in exchanges about the boundaries of acceptable Jewish self-representation and self-criticism.[26] Only those debates often turned on literature. Philip Roth's work, for example, played a key part in them.[27] Today, "Jewish self-hatred" tends to be used in the political sector of the public sphere, and like so much of what is said there, it has gone viral.

Since 2000, the website http.masada2000.org has kept a list of "self-hating Israeli traitors," which includes politically moderate American Jews who believe that Israel is, to some degree, responsible for the severity of the Arab-Israeli conflict.[28] The tag "Jewish self-hatred" figures centrally, moreover, in David Mamet's book *The Wicked Son* (2005); under that rubric, Mamet anathematizes (mostly unnamed) Jews "whose denunciations of Israel," in his opinion, "rise to the realm of race treason."[29] In this general context, Rush Limbaugh, too, deployed the label "self-hating Jew," though he had a more specific target—George Soros.[30] The same goes for Benjamin Netanyahu, the prime minister himself, whose objects of opprobrium in 2009 were Rahm Emanuel and David Axelrod.[31]

Thus a number of Jewish public figures and intellectuals have felt pressed, during the past decade, to rebut the charge that their criticisms of Israel stem from a self-destructive self-loathing.[32] In a 2007 issue of the British newspaper *The Guardian*, for instance, Jacqueline Rose denies that Jewish self-hatred is what has prompted her to scrutinize and speak out against various aspects of Israel's political culture. But Rose did more than defend herself; she also went on the attack, campaigning against the "myth of Jewish self-hatred." The late historian Tony Judt did likewise. A frequent contributor to the *New York Review of Books*, Judt used that forum to call for a binational Israeli state, as well as to condemn Israel's treatment of its Arab citizens. And 2007 saw him censure his censurers, some of whom had tried to link his positions on Israel to Jewish self-hatred and "inner" antisemitism. Judt warned that when Jews (and non-Jews) who stay within the parameters of reasonable debate are made out to be antisemites, concepts on which many people rely lose their value. The risk, he admonished, is that every "reference to anti-Semitism" will come across as another "political defense of Israeli policy."[33]

No wonder, then, that the skepticism of today's critics of "Jewish self-hatred" often surpasses Janik's. Janik never recommended that we banish the rubric from scholarly discourse. Indeed, he praised what may well be the two most notable analytic appropriations of the term: Kurt Lewin's "classic," "sophisticated" article "Self-Hatred among Jews" (1941), and Sander Gilman's "magisterial" study *Jewish Self-Hatred* (1986).[34] A commentator writing in the Israeli newspaper *Ha'aretz*, by contrast, recently declared "Jewish self-hatred" to be "a bogus concept."[35] Similarly, in his review of *The Anti-Journalist* (2008), my book about Karl Kraus, the Germanist R. C. Conard all but insists that no scholar has ever managed to work fruitfully with "Jewish self-hatred." Conard gives a very short sketch of the term's career, which he sees as filled with fraud: "for many years the expression 'Jewish self-hatred' has passed as coinage in the realm of scholarship."[36] From there, Conard goes on to wish that "this cheap psychological currency will lose all claim to academic legitimacy."[37] Never mind that some of the leading lights in Jewish studies—for example, Paul Mendes-Flohr , Todd Endelman, and Shulamit Volkov—have employed the category "Jewish self-hatred" with a high degree of self-awareness.[38] Never mind, as well, that in doing so their intention has been to delineate historical patterns of self-fashioning among German Jews, rather than to put forth compromising psychological diagnoses.

In the most extensive genealogy of "Jewish self-hatred" published during the past ten years, the psychologist Mick Finlay harbors hopes much like Conard's, while underscoring a connection that Janik left untouched. Finlay's essay "Pathologizing Dissent" (2005) lays out a trajectory whereby Zionist "identity politics" have determined the concept's course. The notion was imbued with political (and polemical) meanings at the very beginning, according to Finlay, and they have kept their place at its core. "Jewish self-hatred" has retained its element of identity politics even in academic projects like Gilman's, which, in Finlay's view, winds up promoting "normative definitions of Jewish identity."[39]

As Gilman presents them, his aims don't play to such ends. Gilman's is, to a large extent, a literary critical or "tropological" endeavor, as he puts it, signaling that he will be bringing to bear on his subject the methods of discourse analysis. But Gilman's starting point is a piece of psychology. Gilman takes the phenomenon of Jewish self-hatred to be like other minority self-hatreds. For him, these result "from the outsiders' acceptance of the mirage of themselves generated by their reference group—that group in society which they see as defining them—as a reality."[40] Equipped with this conception of the self-hater's confusion, Gilman sets about trying to understand how the trope of the Jews' linguistic inferiority came to pervade German-Jewish letters, even as they so forcefully gave the lie to it. In doing so, Gilman, if anything, normalizes Jewish self-hatred. For he finds it everywhere: in Moses Mendelssohn, Heine, Börne, Marx, Berthold Auerbach, Kafka, and Kraus, among many others. It may even be that Gilman's study, which appeared around the same time as Janik's article, draws on the frustration that Janik flagged as his impetus—that is, the frustration over seeing "Jewish self-hatred" used to dismiss German-Jewish authors as unserious.

But regardless of whether or not Finlay's "Pathologizing Dissent" is fair in its assessment of Gilman's book, the genealogy that Finlay puts forward has obvious shortcomings. One is that it is too selective: Finlay simply passes over the many instances of "Jewish self-hatred" that don't jibe with the story he wants to tell. Another weakness is that his genealogy is, in a way, too inclusive. Much of the time, the apparent goal of Finlay's undertaking is to develop a historical critique of a specific conceptual pair, namely, "self-hating Jew" and "Jewish self-hatred." Hence his subtitle: "Zionism, Identity Politics, and the 'Self-hating Jew.'" And, indeed, as Finlay looks for lines of semantic continuity running from Lessing, through Lewin and Gilman, to debates about Israel in the present day, he suggests that the accumulated resonances of "the term self-hate" pull its users toward identity politics. Yet in dealing with the term's early history, Finlay treats words whose meanings seem close to that of "Jewish self-hatred" as though they denoted and connoted exactly what "Jewish self-hatred" did. Often, in fact, he implies that he is talking about the use of that particular locution, when he is alluding to an occurrence of something else, for example, "Jewish antisemitism."[41]

Thus Finlay leaves us with the impression that a series of Zionist and anti-Zionist authors, including Lessing, started to speak of "Jewish self-hatred" well before the concept became part of their lexicon.[42] Doing this helps Finlay. It is what allows him to posit that Zionists and their Jewish critics brought the phrase "Jewish self-hatred" into currency just as they were beginning to discredit each other in the harshest of keys, or at the fin de siècle.[43] By not distinguishing between "Jewish self-hatred" and the similar-sounding labels that preceded it, Finlay, in other words, gives (undue) added weight to his argument about the links between the advent of Zionist identity politics and the origins of "Jewish self-hatred." Yet we shouldn't reduce this strategy to an effect of Finlay's axe-to-grind style of historical reconstruction. The authors of the most influential genealogies of "Jewish self-hatred" have made the same move, after all, and they have held to the term as an analytic category. With them, the practice of nondistinction hasn't furthered programmatic ends. It is just a way of doing conceptual history.

III

Conceptual history and other kinds of history are, as Reinhart Koselleck has pithily put it, "different."[44] Exactly how they differ will have to remain a question for another day. What bears mentioning here is that like all areas of history, conceptual history poses its own special challenges, and genealogists of "Jewish self-hatred" haven't given all of them the attention they deserve. I'm thinking, in particular, of the challenge of linguistic resemblance. Let's say you've written a so-cial history of the First World War. Perhaps you've found a way to dispute how previous authors have set the temporal boundaries of your topic. But how far will you have gone? In all likelihood, you won't have staked your career on the claim that although appearances suggest otherwise, the Great War began with the Franco-Prussian conflict of 1870. So as you read through the proofs of your book, catching many flaws you can no longer fix, you'll at least be spared the feeling that you've managed to conflate your event with a much earlier one.

But a practitioner of conceptual history could easily have just that experience. If she's not doing traditional *Begriffsge-schichte*, which tends to begin with etymological tracking and then to follow an individual key term, there's a good chance that a person delving into conceptual history will be seeking, in effect, to understand the formation of a discourse. Along the way, it could well seem that a part of the discourse—even the concept ostensibly at issue—emerged before it really did, because by the time the part came to be, its larger discursive setting had come together. Imagine a scenario where a concept hasn't quite arrived in its mature form, but people have been talking more or less about what the concept would mean, in terms much like the ones in which the concept ultimately would be cast. The general notion of X has gained currency; the specific locution "X" hasn't yet been coined. If the (often unspoken) goal is to comprehend a discursive turn, rather than a rhetorical twist, then why dwell on the gap between currency and coinage? Why even stop to mark it?[45]

A tour of the prehistory of "Jewish self-hatred" should help us see why the concept's discourse-oriented genealogists have overlooked or brushed aside such questions. Precursor terms and discussions begin to occur as far back as the Enlightenment era. In pondering the Jews' suitability for civic emancipation, the philosopher Lazarus Bendavid worried that oppression had made his people into a "nation of slaves," whose peculiarities included a surfeit of self-contempt.[46] These thoughts of 1793 amount, according to one critic, to "practically a theory of Jewish self-hatred."[47] We might also say that about Rahel Varnhagen's self-analyses, which date from Bendavid's day. Rahel, as she is generally called, was born in 1771, in Berlin, to affluent parents. Legendarily quick-witted, and full of passion for German letters, she founded a salon in the family home while still in her teens. It was an immediate success; by the mid-1790s, the gatherings Rahel hosted attracted some of Berlin's most dynamic minds.

After a hiatus, during which she married the Prussian diplomat Karl August Varnhagen von Ense and converted to Protestantism, Rahel restarted her salon in the 1820s. This time, too, she was able to bring together many of the most vibrant intellects of the day, like Hegel and Heine. But although Rahel reached a level of integration that would have been unthinkable during her own childhood, she spent much of her life feeling bitter about her fate. It wasn't simply that the antisemitic barbs she had to endure wounded her, or that they made for a position that would remain odd and tantalizing, even as it became a familiar one among the German-Jewish literati: being both insider and outsider. In letters and conversations recorded by her husband, Rahel at once voices and probes the type of internecine resentment that the psychologist Lewin, as a German-Jewish émigré, would put at the center of the seminal work mentioned above, "Self-Hatred among Jews." Indeed, Rahel took large steps toward anticipating basic aspects of Lewin's essay, which, with a nod to Lessing, helped introduce the term "Jewish self-hatred" to the Anglo-American public sphere.[48]

Lewin wrote about how stereotypes and discrimination could lead those members of an "underprivileged group" who sought social acceptance to blame, in effect, the victim, and despise their own background as the cause of their unhappiness. More than a century earlier, Rahel luridly parsed how she experienced her Jewish descent as a shameful, soul-killing stain that couldn't be washed away, and that, along with her status as a woman, prevented her from flourishing as nature had equipped her to. "My whole life," she once reflected, "is a process of bleeding to death."[49]

Rahel died in 1833. By then, frustrations like hers had become more widespread within the fast-changing German-Jewish community; and when, not long thereafter, a new form of German-Jewish literature emerged, it soon yielded further evocations of Jewish self-hatred. Amid much else, the 1830s and 1840s witnessed the rise of what Jonathan Hess has called "German-Jewish middlebrow fiction."[50] Written to a large extent by rabbis, and for the growing ranks of Jewish readers of German, this literature promoted both acculturation and devotion to Judaism. These goals were seen as compatible and even as complementary—by both reform and orthodox authors. But both variants of German-Jewish middlebrow fiction also came with warnings. Acculturation could be dangerous: if pursued the wrong way, it would lead to psychological problems, chief among them something like Jewish self-hatred.

Consider the novella *Advancement and Hindrance* (1841), by the liberal rabbi Ludwig Philippson. Serialized in the *Allgemeine Zeitung des Judentums*, the newspaper Philippson had helped launch in 1837, it stages precisely the sort of caveat I've just described. The story begins with an account of a conversation: our two middle-aged male protagonists meet while vacationing at a spa, where they soon find themselves discussing how being Jewish has affected them. One of the characters is the narrator, and he quickly expresses misgivings about the dialogue. He tells Bernhard, his interlocutor, that the two of them shouldn't hold themselves apart from the mostly non-Jewish group at the spa. Soon they will stand out—in a bad way. With their talk of Jewish topics, they will draw negative attention to themselves, and be left only with each other, a community of two. This has already happened, Bernhard rejoins. Hasn't their waiter made a point of being slow in serving them? Shouldn't they see the waiter's behavior as a message basically telling them: don't feel as welcome as your fellow guests, because you aren't? The unnamed narrator concedes, dispiritedly, that Bernhard is right.

Thus the novella frames two stories of acculturation, through which we learn that even amidst burgeoning possibility and mobility, Jewish integration isn't a simple matter. Indeed, plenty of "hindrance" remains. Bernhard, the well-adjusted realist, has nevertheless made the most of his situation. He embraced the chance to participate in the efforts of the larger society, fighting, and eventually bleeding, alongside non-Jewish soldiers for the German cause in the Napoleonic wars, something he recalls as a stirring experience. But Bernhard has also remained loyal to the Jewish community: he married a Jewish woman, raised his children in the Jewish faith, and is a dedicated reader of the Old Testament. The result appears to be a productive life and inner contentment.

Bernhard's conversation partner is, by contrast, a desolated figure. Growing up in a small town, the narrator allowed European literature to fire his imagination, and he formed hopes of freedom and possibility. But these set him up only to be waylaid by disappointment. When the narrator went out into the world, and was greeted by old and new prejudices more than acceptance, he wasn't braced for the hurt inflicted upon him. The next major blow hit the narrator even harder, breaking his heart. He relates to Bernhard that he fell deeply in love with a woman who requited every ounce of his ardor, and with whom he bonded over a shared affinity for European literature, which, by now, has begun to come across as a siren's song, rather than as a means of *Bildung*. For the narrator's adoration had as its object a Christian woman, with whom marriage proved untenable. In answering his offer to undergo baptism, she reminded him that the step would bring about a terrible "splitting" and "loss of character." Brittle from despair, and with little faith and no community to support him, the narrator wasn't equal to the challenge of coping with the further discrimination to which he was subjected. And so he started to have the sense that he "deserved" the "contempt" heaped on him "as a Jew." In turn, the narrator developed, as he puts it, "the psychological condition of sincere self-contempt" (*Seelenzustand aufrichtiger Selbstverachtung*).[51]

German-Jewish middlebrow literature shows its Jewish characters taking on antisemitic perspectives in another way as well. In "Prejudgments," a story by Philippson published in 1862, Frau Meyering, a Jewish woman of means and parvenu sensibilities, flies into high dudgeon upon reporting that a bookseller had the audacity to send her free issues of Jewish newspapers. Several things about the bookseller's attempt to hook her as a customer gall Frau Meyering, one of them being that the bookseller evidently thinks of her as a Jew. In her fit of indignation, she brays, "as though I belonged to the 'Jewish people!'"[52] But as Frau Meyering knows, she does belong to the "Jewish people," and the suggestion that she might want to broadcast this unfortunate circumstance by buying and displaying "Jewish writings" also strikes her as offensive. Frau Meyering makes it very clear that hell will freeze over before "I put one of those books on my book table, so that all my guests can see that we are Jews." As a social climber, Frau Meyering wants to be considered tasteful, and, for her, being Jewish and the world of "Jewish affairs" are antithetical to that.

Some figures in German-Jewish middlebrow fiction go even farther than Frau Meyering, in both trying to leave behind their Jewish background and regarding other Jews as a foreign and lowly group. Indeed, some figures conceal their Jewish identity more concertedly, while distancing themselves from other Jews more radically, until, as it generally happens in this didactic body of literature, they recognize the error of their ways. Such is the arc, for example, of the banker Wilhelm Wolfssohn in Marcus Lehmann's novella *To Reap and to Sow* (1870). Not only does Wolfssohn convert to Protestantism, as well as try to hide his past behind the name von Wolfseck, but before coming around to a robust appreciation for his heritage, he also turns his back—eagerly and utterly—on his Jewish family and friends.[53]

Lehmann's allegiances were with rabbi Samson Raphael Hirsch, a brilliant and combative thinker, and with Hirsch's "new" brand of orthodoxy, which strove to be both religiously rigorous and culturally integrationist. And in *To Reap and to Sow*, Lehmann does something orthodox authors of German *belles lettres* often did. He includes a lesson about the perils of another movement started by nineteenth-century German Jews: reform Judaism. Perhaps more than any other factor, reform, which by 1870 had risen to institutional predominance in the German-Jewish community, sets Wolfssohn traveling down the wrong path. *To Reap and to Sow* presents reform as a self-abasing compromise, which is, as such, ultimately self-undermining. Its weak version of Judaism can only fail to inspire and thus to retain a committed following; hence—at least in part—Wolfssohn's apostasy.

It was this outlook that led to the coining of the phrase "Jewish antisemites." Orthodox writers came up with that appellation, and began to enlist it in their pillorying of their German-Jewish rivals, as early as 1882, or just three years after Wilhelm Marr's book *The Victory of Jewry over the Germans* had popularized the term "antisemitism." Pulling out the rhetorical stops, in newspapers like *The Jewish Press* and *The Israelite*, orthodox writers excoriated both "Jewish atheists" and some reform Jews as "Jewish antisemites," as spreaders of "Jewish Jew-hatred," and as "inner enemies," who were harming Judaism more gravely than any outside force could.[54] At the end of the 1890s, another sectarian struggle brought the first of those three phrases into much wider currency. Theodor Herzl's *The Jews' State* (1896), the founding text of political Zionism, castigates those Zionists who challenged the need for, or practicality of, the push for Jewish statehood as "disguised antisemites of Jewish origin."[55] Only a year later, Herzl would complain of how often Jewish anti-Zionists invoked the same language to tar him. They were, as it turned out, just getting started.

In 1898, Karl Kraus's pamphlet *A Crown for Zion* appeared, giving greater visibility to the line that Herzl and his followers were "Jewish antisemites," who, like other antisemites, dwelled on Jewish physical differences and wanted to "get the Jews out of Europe."[56] Well on his way, at the time, to becoming Vienna's best-known satirist, Kraus also quipped that with their appropriation of nationalist ideals, Zionists stood to "make antisemites out of people who have had no patience for such things." He soon announced that they had made one out of him. Writing in 1899, Kraus averred that given his attitude toward the "Jewish tendencies responsible for Zionism," he now belonged among the "antisemitic Jews" and "Jewish antisemites."[57] It seems that Kraus, a dedicated nonconformist and provocateur, was trying to distance himself from the standard use of a term he had done much to make widespread—too widespread, that is, for his taste. By associating his *own* position on Zionism with "Jewish antisemitism," Kraus created a salient contrast between himself and the commentators who enlisted the phrase to impugn *other* Jews for being Zionists or anti-Zionists.

Herzl had already stopped wielding the rubric by then, as far as I can tell.[58] But that Jews suffered from self-contempt remained an important theme in his writings. In underlining this motif, Herzl was, in a way, connecting with a much larger discursive trend, one that Nietzsche's diagnoses of culture had helped inspire—especially Nietzsche's theories of how Western values had turned man against himself and made man tired of himself.[59] Indeed, many thinkers in fin-de-siècle Germany and Austria expressed concerns about what they took to be a modern crisis of nervous self-alienation and existential inauthenticity. And Jewish self-disaffection could, and did, serve as a kind of metaphor for the more general malaise.

Certainly it does in Hermann Bahr's foray into urban history, *Vienna* (1906). Here Bahr, a star critic who had reviewed Herzl's play *The New Ghetto* (1894), laments that Vienna is a place full of people manically trying to shed their true identity and enact a new one. In Bahr's book, the city abounds with pitifully self-disrespecting "hollow shells," and it is in this sense, he writes, that Vienna is "Jewified." Vienna was "already" Jewified "long before the first Jew arrived there," Bahr adds, making it clear that such Jewification doesn't require Jews, or necessarily have anything to do with their influence.[60] Nor did Herzl see self-disdain among Jews as fundamentally Jewish. The problem belongs to *the* Jewish experience, to be sure. But any group subjected to the trials of prolonged exile and discrimination will suffer from auto-animus. As the all-knowing narrator in Herzl's novel *Old-New Land* (1902) puts it, "There are words in every language for the same thing—to be reviled and thus, finally, to revile oneself!"[61] Do away with the external reviling, the novel's images of proud, desert-dwelling Jews imply, and the Jews' self-reviling will go, too.

Meanwhile, however, other writers were penning takes on Jewish self-hatred whose message was that Jews have a special relationship with self-loathing, that self-hatred among Jews is really a *Jewish* self-hatred. The authors of these evocations drew on an array of contemporary discourses, stereotypes, and perceptions, some of which were pitted against each other. There is, for example, the case of Emanuel Schreiber versus Heinrich von Treitschke. When Schreiber, the chief rabbi of Bonn's Jewish community, wrote his book *The*

Self-Criticism of the Jews (1880), he did so as a direct response to Treitschke's screed "Our Prospects" (1879). A well-regarded historian, who is often said to have made antisemitism respectable, Treitschke blamed the Jews for the divisiveness wracking Germany during the *Kulturkampf* period. Or more precisely, he blamed Jewish journalists and the liberal newspapers owned by Jews, the greatest of which—the *Frankfurter Zeitung* and the *Berliner Tageblatt*—had come into being between the 1850s and 1870s. As in Richard Wagner's essay "'Modern'" (1878), which treats "Jewish journalism" as the caustic, destructive, venal force that "introduced modernity" to German culture, in Treitschke's article the "Jewish press" is the dreaded instrument of a hypermodern, hypercritical people. Rootless and ruthless, the Jews hold nothing sacred except their own interests. These qualities make them uniquely well suited for manipulating the flow of mass media: their German competitors appear to have no chance. Thus without the least bit of compunction, the "Jewish press" successfully buries all who dare to cross it, leaving everyone terrified and the public sphere deformed. The "overrepresentation" of Jews in the press is, according to Treitschke, the "most dangerous threat" to Germany's well-being.[62]

Schreiber countered that thanks to the legacy of the prophets and a prizing of intellectual dispute, the Jews have actually specialized in the most unsparing self-reflection. They have been "the classic people of self-criticism," as his opening epigraph has it.[63] But despite the opposition between Treitschke's claims and Schreiber's, it should be easy to imagine how someone might combine elements of the ideas they championed. Indeed, Thomas Mann does this in his story "The Blood of the Walsungs" (1905), which also brings into the mix other tropes that go to underscore the specificity of Jewish self-hatred. Loosely based on the life of Mann's in-laws, the wealthy and accomplished Pringsheims, "The Blood of the Walsungs" threatened to create a scandal in part because of the incest scene with which it ends. And much of what drives the young Aarenhold twins into each other's arms is a pampered, narcissistic scorning of the vulgarity of the outside world. Yet Mann, ever the dialectician, sketches his characters in such a way that the same tendencies that foster feelings of superiority and self-love also engender Jewish self-hatred. In a further twist, Jewish self-hatred turns out to have helped make those tendencies possible.

Born poor in "a remote town in the East," the patriarch of the Aarenhold family amassed a fortune through boldly entering into the coal industry. This seems to have happened during the *Gründerzeit,* a time of rapid industrialization in Germany, which is also when the Jews became fully enfranchised German citizens. The Aarenholds have embraced the moment in a highly stereotypical way. They have poured vast sums into the acquisition of *Deutschtum,* appointing their mansion like a medieval castle, and they have given their progeny ultra-Germanic names. The offspring, for their part, have lived up to this nomenclature. Brought up far away from *shtetl* life, the Aarenholds' children have reached a more advanced stage of acculturation. One of the twins, Sieglinde, has agreed to marry the blond every-German Beckerath. The other, Siegmund, has as his *métier* surrounding himself with the trappings of German high culture. But in various ways— ways both physical and temperamental—the Aarenholds remain different. With his cynicism, his ennui, and his overdetermined mastery of the rules for appropriate evening attire, Siegmund, who wages war against his exotic beard growth, could hardly be more unlike the ingenuous and rumpled civil servant Beckerath. Furthermore, when all four Aarenhold siblings come together with Beckerath and their parents for a meal, the younger Aarenholds' rapid, precocious, Talmudic verbal jousting makes Beckerath's head spin.

Better at breaking down than building up, the Aarenhold siblings are portrayed as "demons of negation," to borrow a phrase that Wagner once applied to Heinrich Heine. Their critical faculties appear to be a point of pride, as well as something they enjoy activating. But since the siblings have been raised to take on the majority culture's standards of respectability, they wind up subjecting the signs and remnants of their own lowly Eastern-Jewish heritage to their outsized, old-new captiousness, which is less fun. Where this happens, Mann's story evokes, or anticipates, Arthur Schnitzler's well-known remark about how "antisemitism didn't become serious until the Jews got ahold of it." Upon listening to their father make a mawkish statement, Herr Aarenhold's children "exchange glances so aggressively that he couldn't help but notice." Herr Aarenhold "knew about his offspring," the narrator tells us, that "they were all against him, that they all despised him: because of his origins, because of the blood that flowed in him and that he had passed on to them, because of how he had come by his wealth. . . . He knew it, and to some extent, he agreed with them."[64] However, Herr Aarenhold also feels that he is due at least a measure of respect. He has managed, after all, to climb high—using precisely the self-hatred of an Eastern Jew. The narrator reports about Herr Aarenhold's self-understanding and his social mobility: "He had been a worm, a louse, yes, indeed. It was just his ability to experience this so fervently and so self-contemptuously that was behind the tenacious and insatiable striving, which, ultimately, had brought about his rise."[65]

By the time "The Blood of the Walsungs" got Mann into some hot water, a new breed of German-Jewish authors—call them modernists—had begun to explore the theme of assimilation and its discontents in a decidedly nondidactic way. Schnitzler, for example, had misgivings about Zionism, but in his great novel about the Jewish Question, his chief commitment is to an uncompromising psychological realism, and this agenda yielded diverse representations of self-enmity. If several characters touch on the idea that Zionists and antisemites share certain anti-Jewish prejudices, the most stridently anti-Jewish Jewish character in Schnitzler's *The Road into the Open* (1908) is appalled by his father's Zionist sympathies. Not only that, the figure who most closely resembles Schnitzler, the splenetic playwright Heinrich Bermann, is also opposed to Zionism, and he strikes the novel's non-Jewish protagonist as being "a worse antisemite than most of the Christians I know."[66] It was because of these ruminations that Lewin counted Schnitzler among the early analysts of Jewish self-hatred.[67]

Lewin might have included Freud, Schnitzler's fellow Viennese, among them as well. Writing, in 1905, about the "phobia of a five-year-old," Freud postulated that the "deepest root of antisemitism is the castration complex." "Already in their nurseries," Freud asserts in a footnote," "little boys learn that the Jew loses a piece of his penis, and this gives them the right to despise him."[68] But what begins as a theory of antisemitism quickly develops into an account of Jewish antisemitism, however compact and implicit it may be. For Freud supports his point about the origins of Jew-hatred by referring his readers to the case of none other than Weininger, a notoriously anti-Jewish Jew. The intimation, we might even say, is that Jewish men have a special reason for having a castration complex, and thus for being antisemitic. To be sure, Freud describes Weininger simply as a "neurotic," not as a Jewish one. Yet at the very least Freud leaves readers to wonder why this particular neurotic, whose Jewish background was well known, would so clearly bring to light the link between antisemitism and castration anxiety. Why was Weininger the neurotic who, in Freud's words, "thought of Jews and woman with the same sense of abhorrence," and "vituperated against them in the same way?"[69]

Years later, Freud gave an answer. It was 1933, and Hitler's rise had motivated Freud to engage more expansively with the mechanisms behind what he called the "undying hatred the Jews had attracted." And this time, too, Freud wound up producing a reading of Jewish self-hatred. In a letter dated August 18, 1933, he remarks to his friend Arnold Zweig, "One defends oneself in every way against the fear of castration. Here a piece of opposition to one's own Jewishness may still be hiding cunningly. Our great master Moses was, after all, strongly antisemitic. Perhaps he really was an Egyptian."[70] These ruminations were work in progress, and as Freud kneaded his idea about Moses's heritage into the shape of a thesis—that is, the thesis of his last book, *Moses and Monotheism* (1938)—he added quite a bit to his thinking about Jewish self-hatred. In Freud's retelling of the Moses story, the Jews' early culture of auto-antipathy becomes far more radical than the one featured in the biblical version. What makes for the difference is precisely the turning of Moses into an outsider. In his "Moses book," Freud writes of Moses's typical Egyptian "contempt" for the "inferior" Jewish people. This Egyptian Moses feels himself to be "stooping" to the depths in his attempt to lift up the Jews. "Our great leader Moses" is, indeed, "strongly antisemitic," yet not because he associates circumcision with castration, and the Jews exacerbate his castration anxiety. Rather, Freud now stresses that Moses brought circumcision to the Jews, so now Moses looks down on the Jews for *not* being circumcised, for lacking the key sign of civilized faith.[71]

The Jews, for their part, see Moses and the ideals that are the cornerstones of Judaism from the perspective of suspicious outsiders—as how could they not? Freud has put them in that role. If the founder of Judaism hates the Jews as a lesser, alien folk, the Jews loathe their founder and his anti-instinctual spirituality as other people would come to. In effect, the Jews are at once the first followers of Judaism and the first people to experience it as a foreign threat. Thus the Jews become, in Freud's narrative, self-lacerating in a way that goes well beyond the self-chastising of the prophets. In a word, the

Jews display Ur-antisemitism—just as much as Moses does—and their rage against him and his Jewishness is much greater than the Bible suggests it is. According to Freud's Moses story, the Jews are the ones who smash the stone tablets, and their rancor toward Moses eventually grows murderous. They kill him, in fact.

By the logic of Freud's book, the Jews' special culture of self-hatred would be carried forth through the generations by mysteriously transmitted "memory traces." Perhaps, then, Freud had this newly excavated culture in mind in 1936, when he asked Kurt Hiller whether there might be something particularly Jewish about Theodor Lessing's self-contempt. "Don't you think," Freud muses in a letter to Hiller, "that self-hatred like Th. L.'s is an exquisite Jewish phenomenon?"[72] In the same letter, on the other hand, Freud tries to understand Lessing's Jewish self-hatred in terms of basic psychoanalytic principles, and he has an easy time of it. Psychoanalysis establishes, at its core, a self-divided against itself; the male child's aggression toward his role model; and the need to adopt the perspective of a more powerful rival. So as we might expect, well before Freud speculated that self-hatred results from a person's "inability to give up either an intense hostility toward his father or an dissoluble identification with the father," to use Peter Gay's handy paraphrasing, thinkers with ties to psychoanalysis had discussed the issue.[73]

Weininger was one of them. Weininger's close friend Hermann Swoboda, who was a patient of Freud's for a time, may well have shared with Weininger some of the new (and not-yet-published) ideas to which therapy was exposing him.[74] These likely included the theory of homosexuality as owing to a universal bisexual stage, for Weininger takes just such a position in *Sex and Character*.[75] The book begins, in fact, with the claim that "sexual differentiation is never complete."[76] It goes on to argue that rather than being a pathology foreign to most people, homosexuality stems from a greater than normal degree of incomplete differentiation.[77] Thus when *Sex and Character* came out in 1903, Freud's early collaborator Wilhelm Fliess felt betrayed, and he angrily accused Freud of the indiscretion that Freud had perhaps committed. But Weininger didn't stop at bisexuality. Applying the same sort of logic to the matter of Jewish identity, he hypothesized that the most non-Jewish among us generally have within themselves "elements" of Jewishness. This, in turn, is how *Sex and Character* attempts to make sense of antisemitism. Here antisemitism and Jewish self-hatred amount to the same thing. Weininger stresses that even the antisemitism of his idol Richard Wagner, "the greatest man since Christ," had as its source a well-founded antipathy toward the Jewishness within him. That is, Wagner's hatred of the Jews represents a projecting of self-hatred.[78] And the Jew who hates the "Jewish essence" is merely doing likewise, in Weininger's view. As he puts it, "We only hate others who remind us *un*pleasantly of ourselves."[79]

Not long after *Sex and Character* was published, Fritz Wittels, a member of Freud's Viennese circle, joined the conversation about Jewish self-hatred. Weininger's spectacular suicide—he killed himself in 1903, in the house where Beethoven had lived—was probably a factor in this. But Wittels also thought that he was witnessing in Vienna an epidemic of apostasies, which were being undertaken for all the wrong reasons, namely, greed and shame. And in 1904, this perception, above all, moved Wittels to write a pamphlet about the conniving, self-degrading mentality of such converts.[80] Commonly translated as *The Baptized Jew*, the original title of his work is more starkly censorious. Wittels used the compound noun *Taufjude*; and whereas the phrase "baptized Jew" frames baptism as a discrete action, which may or may not reveal a lot about someone's character, *Taufjude* implies that baptism is an unwholesome distinguishing feature. Indeed, the meaning of *Taufe* (baptism) in *Taufjude* (baptism Jew) bears affinities with that of *Geld* (money) in the unkind expression *Geld-jude* (money Jew), which didn't signify "Jew who has money," so much as "Jew whose world is money." That most words consisting of another noun and *Jude*—from the old epithet "court Jew" to Theodor Lessing's 1901 formulation "intellect Jew"—had a derogatory ring would have added to the harshness of Wittels's term.

At the fin de siècle, Lessing, too, helped to build up the general discourse of Jewish self-hatred, while doing nothing to soften its tone. Born in 1874 to assimilationist parents, Lessing, by his own admission, internalized much of their outlook. He even felt during his childhood in Hanover that being Jewish was "evil," and at a tender age, he resolved to dedicate himself to pursuing the "ideals of *Deutschtum*," as he would later put it.[81] But Lessing soon grew to be a rebellious young intellectual who abominated his father's values and way of life. And shortly after he had split with the antisemitic philosopher Ludwig Klages, the soul mate of his youth, Lessing decided that affecting Germanic airs was "in poor taste." Having converted to Protestantism in 1895, Lessing began, a few years later, to reach out to his Jewish heritage. In 1901, he started to identify with Zionism and to write about the Jewish Question.[82]

It was, however, a rude embrace. This was in keeping with the moment. Like quite a few Zionist literati of his generation, Lessing catalogued the faults of his fellow Jews far more zestfully than he celebrated Jews, Jewishness, or Jewish culture. Fueled by Oedipal outrage, schooled on the broodings of Schopenhauer and Nietzsche, and enamored of Martin Buber but still inclined to see Jews in the worst light, Lessing's natural focus was the (perceived) psychic disrepair that made cultural Zionism and its promise of inner renewal seem so necessary. It was in this spirit that Lessing began to hold forth on what he regarded as the pretentious, pettifogging, overly

cerebral, and generally self-diminishing ways of the acculturated Jewish literati. Hence the tag "intellect Jews."[83] Using it,
Lessing assailed figures like the critic Samuel Lublinski for
squandering their talents, and thus degrading themselves,
through their particular style of cultural striving. Unlike
Buber, moreover, Lessing didn't look to Eastern Jews for an
alternative model of Jewishness. He believed that they, too,
had fallen into an execrable condition, and in the years before the First World War, Lessing wrote witheringly about
both Western Jewry and *Ostjuden*. As he would allow in his
memoir, his goal back then was to be *the* "scourge of Jewish
degeneration."[84]

Lessing worked toward that end with such truculence that
he appeared to partake of some of the very syndromes he
wanted to expose. It didn't help that Lessing sometimes oper-
ated in a satirical mode, putting forth caricatures of assimilation that crossed the line, according to quite a few commentators, including, ironically enough, Thomas Mann. By 1910, as
a result, Lessing had gained a reputation for being a Jewish
antisemite.[85]

Lessing also brought to his task a journalist's penchant for
terminological variety, and in both his correspondence and
his caustic essays on "intellect Jews" like Lublinski, we find a
panoply of phrases that may seem almost synonymous with
the one for which he is known today.[86] Indeed, decades before
his "Jewish self-hatred book" appeared, Lessing wrote of Jewish "self-censuring,"[87] "self-torturing,"[88] and "self-betrayal,"[89]
as well as of the Jews' "self-contempt,"[90] and their "lack of self-
respect"[91] and "self-esteem."[92]

It appears to make some sense, then, to see the notion
"Jewish self-hatred" as the child of fin-de-siècle discourse
networks, which is what a press in Germany did in 2007,
when it published Lessing's 1913 profile of the philosopher
Georg Simmel under the new title *Intellect and Self-Hatred*. It

is also what the best-known genealogists of "Jewish self-hatred" have done. For example, in a section of his study titled "The Development of the Concept of Jewish Self-Hatred," Sander Gilman claims that "the merging of the image of the self-critical Jew with that of the mad Jew produced, in the final decades of the nineteenth century, the image of the self-hating Jew as part of the rhetoric of race."[93] While Gilman's attempt to date the coining of the concept breaks off there, this general line of argumentation doesn't. For Gilman goes on to point up the fin-de-siècle provenance of "Jewish self-hatred" by emphasizing how much Lessing's book of 1930 perpetuated conceptual and rhetorical trends that had been in place for quite a while. He contends, in fact, that Lessing's *Jewish Self-Hatred* basically retrains a lens Lessing had made use of back in 1909, in a series of dispatches on the moral and material state of *Ostjuden* in Galicia. According to Gilman, those earlier efforts and Lessing's book rely on "much the same paradigm." This, ostensibly, is why Lessing's *Jewish Self-Hatred* gets so little attention in Gilman's genealogy, or about a page of summary and analysis, much of which underlines the book's debt to fin-de-siècle culture. Gilman at once reiterates and tinkers with his chronology in his endnotes, stating there that the "phrase 'Jewish self-hatred' was popularized by Theodor Lessing, *Der jüdische Selbsthaß* . . . but is rooted in work done in Germany before World War I."[94]

Shulamit Volkov, an important voice in Jewish studies, has gone further still in stressing how much the concept "Jewish self-hatred" owes to the prewar scene. In her recent "Excursus on Self-Hatred and Self-Criticism" (2006), she maintains that when Lessing's study appeared, his topic was "already somewhat dated," while his key term was already well worn.[95] Indeed, she asserts that the rise to prominence of "Jewish self-hatred" was an emblematically fin-de-siècle phenomenon. Volkov writes about the rubric that its "prevalent use was typical of a certain particular phase in the history of German Jews, following the completion of their formal emancipation, especially during the years immediately preceding World War I."[96]

IV

It turns out, however, that "Jewish self-hatred" enjoyed neither prevalence nor prominence before the Great War. Even with new word-search capabilities lending a very fast helping hand, the earliest instance I could find dates from 1921.[97] While it may be that the concept had already been coined—and become a staple of oral discussions—I have my doubts. After all, Kraus, who had his language-obsessed ear to the ground for such things, didn't speak of "Jewish self-hatred" until that same year. But at issue here is much more than chronological correctness. In the case of "Jewish self-hatred," linguistic resemblance hasn't simply been misleading, it has been profoundly so; and we might say about Gilman and Volkov more or less what Nietzsche said about genealogists of morals. They have missed the dialectical movement of their object. Gilman and Volkov conflate "Jewish self-hatred" with a host of terms that seem analogous to it, seeing its origins and its Ur-meanings as nearly identical with theirs; and the two scholars read Lessing's book, among other works, accordingly. Yet in truth, "Jewish self-hatred" was forged to *oppose* those terms. Let me be more precise: I want to argue that "Jewish self-hatred" entered public debate as part of a thoroughly, indeed, self-consciously *post*–World War I undertaking, whose aim was to reorient the existing discourse of Jewish self-hatred. The specific category "Jewish self-hatred" was coined and first applied as a kind of oppositional measure, as a sort of counterconcept.[98]

When Lessing introduced the term into his vocabulary, he was picking up on this shift and the positive, even redemptive meanings that went along with it. Often characterized as a "polemic," Lessing's *Jewish Self-Hatred* actually comes close to being a self-help book, where your sufferings give you opportunities for self-transcendence and improving the world.[99] Certainly the work stands much nearer to the genre of self-help than anything Lessing produced either before it or afterward, when the concept "Jewish self-hatred" all but disappeared from his writings. In 1930, Lessing was struggling to finish his autobiography, and perhaps he thought that he would have better luck imparting his life lessons in a different format. Perhaps he wanted to experiment in another way, too. Maybe he wanted to see whether he could plausibly revise the cultural pessimism in which he often dealt, and, for a change, give German Jewry a bit of much-needed uplift. Or maybe it was a combination of those things that motivated him. Whatever the case, in *Jewish Self-Hatred* Lessing, more than ever before, embraces the idiom and prescriptions of self-help writing. And what I am proposing is that the rubric he chose to foreground there wasn't selected arbitrarily from a group of synonyms, or merely because it was the pithiest or most euphonious of them.[100]

Lessing, in all likelihood, opted for the phrase "Jewish self-hatred" because its original meaning was such that it suited his purposes and fit his *affirmative* message better than any of the terms he had been using, such as "Jewish self-contempt."[101] Neither earlier nor later, after all, did Lessing so concertedly sound lines like these: "Whoever does not love himself will be loved by no one"; "do not run from your destiny"; "love your destiny"; "follow your destiny"; "there are questions that never find a solution—except through a strong resolution"; and, to cite one more example, "be whatever you are, and always try to live up to your best potential."[102] By contrast, in the earlier text Lessing referred to as "his chief statement on the Jewish Question," he conjectures, "Today's Jewry in Western Europe is a non-Jewry that is probably too far gone to be saved by Zionism."[103] An essay from 1932 accepts, and even declares, that the "Jewish Question is unsolvable."[104]

That Lessing forayed into the genre of self-help, while shrewdly promising readers that he would still be taking them "deep into the deep," is also what finally explains the rapturous welcome the self-hatred study got from its Zionist reviewers.[105] Isn't their emphasis on the book's practical value, on how it might heal, how it might open "new perspectives on a great Jewish future," and thus "help set free?" Hence, too, the review in the liberal *Berliner Tageblatt*, which calls Lessing "Buddha's heir." People didn't say analogous things about Lessing's earlier reflections on Western Jewry's "self-splitting" and "self-humiliation" because the prospect of spiritual freedom is hardly the point there. In those fin-de-siècle writings, Lessing generally doesn't hold out much hope that Jews will overcome their characteristic superabundance of self-censuring, which, in his view, had fostered their critical acuity, but also caused chronic, seemingly insurmountable psychic duress.

Of the different conditions that Lessing describes under the heading "Jewish self-hatred," all are painful, too, to be sure. None seems desirable, or even tenable, as a permanent state. Indeed, Lessing warns that some forms of Jewish self-hatred will "leave you dead."[106] Yet there is in his book an existential predicament that takes shape as the chief connotation of "Jewish self-hatred," and *this* Jewish self-hatred comes with big twists. For one thing, it can develop into a kind of "genius" mentality—*der geniale Selbsthaß*, in Lessing's phrasing.[107] For another, it is a problem that will solve itself and then some, if acted upon properly. As in Jacques Derrida's famous reading of the Greek term "*pharmakon*," the poisoning agent turns out to be the cure.[108] Or more specifically, the poison that is Jewish self-hatred, which has done so much to alienate Jews from the joys of material life, is also, in the end, what will enable them to transcend their psychologically precarious situation. But the upside of Jewish self-hatred extends even further. Lessing sees Jewish self-hatred as the most advanced variant of a ubiquitous ill, the curing of which represents the "greatest challenge humanity faces today."[109] And because of the special status of the Jews' self-hatred, Lessing reasons, the Jews are uniquely well positioned to save the world—to lead the world out of and away from self-hatred, and into a better future.

This is, of course, idiosyncratic stuff. Yet as intimated, Lessing's theories owe a lot to the work of someone else, someone very much in his orbit: the largely forgotten Viennese journalist Anton Kuh. Like Lessing, Kuh was a feud-prone German Jew who wore many hats, and whose writings lend themselves, in part for that reason, to being quoted out of context. Kuh was a satirist, an eroticist, an expressionist, a feuilletonist, an activist of sorts, and a celebrated public speaker, known for dazzling audiences with monologues held extemporaneously. His love of and skills at linguistic showmanship have their roots in turn-of-the-century Vienna's coffeehouse culture, where how you spoke could matter a lot more than what you said. But while Kuh was very much at home in that culture, he was, in diverse ways, also a rebel or "outsider" there, as Max Brod put it.[110] Kuh pushed certain bohemian tendencies to extremes; with some justification, he dubbed himself the "king of the shnorrers." Yet from early on in his career, he showed himself to be seriously concerned with the problem of injustice, and he took language seriously, too. For all his verbal playfulness and his much-noted prolixity, Kuh believed in the power of words to do both good and ill. "Terminology is the root of all unhappiness," he once wrote, mingling, as he often did, sincerity and hyperbole.[111] Kuh wasn't "a court jester; he was a jester of the revolutions," one contemporary observed.[112]

Indeed, the First World War radicalized Kuh more than it did many literati of his ilk, and unlike his friend Joseph Roth, who pined for the late-Habsburg "world of yesterday," Kuh welcomed the tumultuous postconflict moment as one of utopian possibility. As Kuh wrote of his mindset toward the end of the conflict, "The pendulum of the revolutionary imagination swung wide during those depressing nights, and the more hopeless they became, the more daring our intellectual hopes grew."[113] But the daring didn't stop with the thought that poison gas and millions of casualties might ultimately help to usher in a better era; it carried over to Kuh's mode of critical analysis as well. Kuh emerged from the war suspicious of all traditional structures of power, having been influenced by an anarchist expressionism that had only just taken shape. Now a committed antinationalist, Kuh also found inspiration in both Nietzsche's broadsides against Prussian self-aggrandizement and in the glee with which Nietzsche belittled things German, in other words, Nietzsche's negative chauvinism. And thus Kuh's 1921 book *Jews and Germans* has as one of its epigraphs Nietzsche's line, "The German race is responsible for everything that has gone wrong with culture."

The year 1921—to the best of my knowledge, it was then that Kuh brought "Jewish self-hatred" into being. But more importantly, it was then that Kuh brought the formulation into being to the best of his own knowledge, for the perception that he was coining the concept is what allowed Kuh to package "Jewish self-hatred," in *Jews and Germans*, as a new term for a new time—as both a reflection and an agent of change.[114] Why the need for a discursive shift? Kuh argued that the Great War revealed, among many other things, the advantages of the poorly understood, much-misrepresented, potentially antinationalist phenomenon that he proposed to rechristen (and reconceptualize) as "Jewish self-hatred." In his construal of it, "Jewish self-hatred" denotes at once an affliction and an existential option. Jewish self-hatred isn't the easiest path for Jews to follow. Still, it is the best way open to them, far better than Zionism and assimilationism, both of which, according to Kuh, would lead Jews further into the disaster of nationalism.

What the Jews need to do is choose their self-hatred, the world's oldest, ripest, and most severe self-hatred. They need to embrace their self-hatred, to activate it productively. Only in this way, paradoxically, will the Jews solve the problem of Jewish self-hatred. And in doing so, they could also achieve much more than that. They could set an example for the rest of humanity, which might prompt it to get beyond its self-hatred and, in the process, overcome a network of related blights, like nationalism, and sexual and political oppression. Another of the epigraphs that introduce *Jews and Germans* comes from the nineteenth-century German-Jewish writer Ludwig Börne, and evokes something of the dialectics that Kuh had in mind to promote with his new term. The passage reads, "The Jews stand much closer to freedom than the German. They are slaves, and one day they will break their chains and be truly free. The German is a servant. He could be free, but doesn't want to be." So here, at the likely moment of its formation, we find the concept "Jewish self-hatred" signaling a sort of messianic promise, even more than a self-abnegating outlook.[115] Or we might say that the term's very reason for being was to express both meanings at once, to function almost like what Freud deemed an *Urwort*, which simultaneously signifies opposing ideas.[116]

If the early history of "Jewish self-hatred" has been misrepresented and thus cries out for recovery, the emergence of the term conforms, in a way, to a familiar pattern. Or so my argument implies. If I am broadly right, then rather than being anonymously produced by big fin-de-siècle discursive trends, "Jewish self-hatred" arrived on the cultural scene as the result of the dynamic interaction between complex contexts of debate and complex German-Jewish figures. It follows that our challenge in writing the genealogy of "Jewish self-hatred" is much like the one we would face if, say, we wanted to make sense of how Freud's *Moses and Monotheism* and its odd content (Moses as an Egyptian!) happened. Accordingly, in the next chapters individual narratives of development will play an important role, and conceptual genealogy will often look like intellectual biography. Our story, in fact, begins with Kuh's story.

V

But before turning to that, I want to touch on what else we stand to gain by revisiting and revising the genealogy of "Jewish self-hatred." One consequence of the perceptions that Janik and Finlay have helped to establish is, in a word, pressure. Scholars who use the concept "Jewish self-hatred" feel pressure to distinguish their application of it from what they see as a long tradition of rebarbative misuse, a tradition that began when the term was born. As a result, definitions of "Jewish self-hatred" are sometimes overcautious, or too restrictive to be of much value. Consider how in a relatively recent essay on German-Jewish hyper-assimilationism, the historian Todd Endelman attempts to delimit the meaning of "Jewish self-hatred." Having labeled Lessing's book a "polemic," and having stressed that since the book's publication, the concept "Jewish self-hatred" has often been misappropriated, both in and beyond academic settings, Endelman wagers the following corrective:

> Self-hating Jews were converts, secessionists, and radical assimilationists who, not content with disaffiliation from the community, felt compelled to articulate how far they had traveled from their origins by echoing antisemitic views, by proclaiming their distaste for those

from whom they wished to dissociate themselves. What set them apart from other radical assimilationists was that, having cut their ties, they were unable to move on and forget their Jewishness.[117]

Though Endelman's goal of greater rigor is laudable, his definition has the drawback of being impractical. How many converted German Jews were allowed to "move on and forget" their Jewishness? And what German Jew actually meets Endelman's remaining criteria? Certainly not the figures Endelman himself names: Rahel Varnhagen, Walther Rathenau, and Jakob Wassermann, the last of whom had ties to the cultural Zionist movement and publicly fretted over how deracination had sapped Jewry's vital intellectual strengths.

If there is good reason to feel uneasy about the term "Jewish self-hatred," scholars who have become attached to the concept needn't worry that it is about to lose its place in academic discourse. Endelman says that he isn't yet ready to give up on the phrase, making it seem as though most scholars have, in fact, moved on. But terminological change is a tricky matter, and categories that cause their users discomfort frequently manage to stick around (even when well-designed alternatives exist). Such is the case with "Jewish self-hatred." Like the notions "assimilation" and "identity," "Jewish self-hatred" appears to be both largely unloved by academics and thoroughly entrenched in academic discourse. My aim, as I hope I've made clear, isn't to defend or rehabilitate the concept, but I would like to think that bringing to light this term's sanguine beginnings—that is, its affirmative early history— will help scholars work with it a little less defensively, and thus more productively.[118]

This, however, isn't to suggest that in the years since Lessing popularized it, "Jewish self-hatred" has been used only to designate something fundamentally dark. There have been other, more positive usages, too, and it may well be that in them we see the past persisting. As Janik emphasized, and as

Koselleck has reminded us, concepts store meanings, which speakers pick up on and perpetuate, often without being fully aware of their role in a process of transmission.[119] Witness Volkov's rather flattering definition of "Jewish self-hatred." In issuing it, Volkov was responding critically to recent appropriations of the term in and beyond German-Jewish studies. She was trying, in other words, to push back against the concept's connotations of pathological self-betrayal. Yet it is also possible—even probable—that Volkov was drawing on historical meanings she had brushed up against, but didn't consciously register, and, thus left out of her genealogy.

Notwithstanding various differences, Volkov sounds quite a bit like Lessing channeling Kuh as she works with "Jewish self-hatred." Its counterpoint, according to her, isn't salutary self-esteem, but rather a dangerous "self-satisfied complacency." Moreover, just as Kuh theorized that the condition of Jewish self-hatred stems from familial dynamics—this is one reason why he chose the word "hatred," which can evoke emotional intimacy—Volkov's account underlines the bond between Jewish self-haters and their targets. Volkov writes about her examples of Jewish self-hatred:

> . . . in their hatred there was love, complex and anguished love. These people, with their open eyes and sharp insights, were the exceptions among the complacent Jews and non-Jews of Wilhelmine society. Such people are always the exceptions.[120]

Although they tend to get lost amidst more clamorous uses of "Jewish self-hatred," there are, in fact, quite a few instances of the term that resonate with the earliest ones, and that we might understand as being part of a tradition of meaning. Indeed, one of the things that sets "Jewish self-hatred" apart from roughly analogous concepts, like "Jewish antisemitism," is that amidst all else it has functioned as a positive point of identification, even as an ideal. When a Zionist rabbi charged the art critic Clement Greenberg (who read Lessing) with being a disloyal, "rootless Jewish intellectual," Greenberg ultimately *defended himself* by insisting that he harbored "Jewish self-hatred," as he put it.[121] In addition to being preferable to the "Jewish chauvinism" of his adversary, "Jewish self-hatred" can be, Greenberg claimed in 1950, quite different from the Jewish self-alienation of which he stood accused. Whereas alienation implies estrangement, "hatred is as intimate a thing as love," Greenberg wrote.

About two decades later, we find Philip Roth picking up on similar connotations. This happens toward the end of *Portnoy's Complaint* (1969), and during a moment of intense anticlimax. Having traveled to Israel to explore his Jewish identity, Alexander Portnoy, the protagonist of the novel, soon sees his way of being Jewish come under attack. More than his unwanted sexual advances, it is Portnoy's self-deprecating *shtick* that sets off Naomi, his main Israeli interlocutor. For him, such self-mockery is a "classic form of Jewish humor." For her, it stinks of the "ghetto." And so Portnoy "disgusts" Naomi. He also angers her. Naomi regards Portnoy's self-questioning manner as "the epitome of what was most shameful in the culture of the Diaspora," and as a fervent Zionist, "the very word Diaspora" makes her "furious." Thus she tells him, "[Y]ou are nothing but a self-hating Jew," whereupon he rejoins, with an air of conviction, "[M]aybe that's the best kind."[122] Kuh might have said the same thing. Actually, he more or less did.

PART TWO

The Birth of "Jewish Self-Hatred" and the Spirit of Interwar Europe

> Nationalism is a spring in which all
> other thoughts turn to sludge.
>
> —KARL KRAUS

Prague, December 30, 1919. As evening grades into night, several hundred people make their way to Smetschkagasse 22, a modern building near Wencelas Square—the site where, a year earlier, Alois Jirásek proclaimed Czech independence. No doubt many of these people have on their minds questions having to do with national identity. But this is more because of the lecture they are about to attend than the neighborhood it happens to be in. They are going to Urania House, a center for German culture, to hear a talk about Western Jewry's plight.

Founded in 1917, Prague's Urania House would eventually host lectures by such stars as the Dadaist Raoul Hausmann and the Nobel Laureate Thomas Mann. Tonight's speaker is much less accomplished. He hasn't played a role in revolutionizing art. Nor has he won even minor awards, let alone prizes of the highest order. Yet for the moment, he has become a sensation of sorts. Indeed, his performance this evening has the character of an encore; newspaper ads boast that the speaker has agreed to return for an extra engagement, so as to sate the popular hunger for one, and that is no sales trick.[1] His lecture "On Sexual Revolution," which he gave at Urania House a few weeks earlier, attracted an overflow crowd.[2] With the same situation taking shape tonight, chairs have been set up on and around the podium where the speaker will stand. The audience will consist, as it did before, mostly of German-Jewish intellectuals—a bookish-seeming lot. But what has brought them out is, at least in part, the speaker's talent for brilliantly and wittily riling his listeners, to the point of creating an atmosphere of highbrow mayhem. Many people will settle into their seats hoping that the speaker will at once provide them with intellectual stimulation and antagonize them, even outrage them. They want the speaker to elicit cheering and jeering, laughter and catcalls. He will prove obliging.

At half-past seven or so, the speaker strides out onto the podium. Not yet thirty, he looks older. In matters of health and hygiene, he is an anti-Kafka—a drinker and smoker, among other things—and it shows. There are deep lines in his face, which is, moreover, pockmarked and drawn, and partially covered by his thick, always unkempt dark hair, his "gypsy-mane," in the parlance of the time. More striking than his features, though, is his bearing. A nervous whip of a man, the speaker doesn't stop walking around in the small space at his disposal. As he moves, he stares at his audience so intently that his eyes seem almost to bulge. A tic, meanwhile, keeps making the speaker's face contract, and his habit of frequently smacking himself on the forehead is as much in effect as ever. Yet even this spectacle is thoroughly overshadowed by the intricate mass of words coming out of the speaker's mouth. His particular gift is for setting language into speech, for being a "*Sprechsteller*," as Kurt Tucholsky once called him, rather than a *Schriftsteller*, or writer.[3]

The provocations begin right away. To an audience in which assimilated Jews predominate, the speaker reveals that his title, "The Tragedy of the Jews," refers primarily to the outcome of Jewish assimilation. Assimilation has failed tragically, he argues, in a number of ways. It is an abject striving that, as such, has helped produce and sustain antisemitism, including the violent form of it that appears to be growing more widespread in Central Europe.[4] In the end, what looms as "the wages" of assimilation is "the pogrom."

Then there is all that gets lost and compromised when Jews "bow their heads before foreign ideals." For a century and a half—from Moses Mendelssohn and his veneration of tolerance, through Ludwig Börne's liberalism, to, worst of all, the patriotism of the Jews who hurried to enlist in 1914—for a century and a half, Jews have taken on local values as a means of establishing themselves within German culture. But despite the many affinities between Germans and Jews, Jews are not of German culture, the speaker insists. A special "Jewish essence," which preceded and shaped Judaism, separates Jews from Germans, as do the Jews' unique historical experiences. So in addition to making the Jews physically unsafe, assimilation has left them self-alienated, or spiritually homeless, as well.

Dilating on the differences between Germans and Jews, the speaker confronts his listeners with a whole series of polarities, such as individualism (Jews) versus fatalism (Germans); sentimental consciousness (Jews) versus naïve absence of self-consciousness (Germans); and can (Jews) versus must (Germans). But the Jewish peculiarity that matters most—the one that gives the Jews their calling—is that they have their homeland precisely in "the souls of other people," which is why Zionism won't help them solve the Jewish Question. What the Jews should do, according to the speaker, is work critically through their dreams of becoming either German nationals or national Jews. In this way, they should start pursuing their "mission" of having—and thus modeling for others—a kind of supranational national identity. Hopefully, the Great War and its menacing aftermath will have helped disillusion Jewish assimilationists. More will be needed, however, to get the Jews to come around, to get them to open themselves up to the real, profoundly ethical Jewishness. And that more entails a climactic paradox, for it means bringing to bear on both assimilationism and Zionism the Jews' brutal style of self-critique. It means, in the speaker's pointed terminology, making productive use of "Jewish antisemitism."[5]

According to Felix Weltsch's review of the lecture, in the Zionist newspaper *Self-Defense*, the speaker caused much excitement and agitation among his mostly non-Zionist Jewish listeners. He even had them scrambling to deliver comebacks from their seats. These scenes amused Weltsch, and for obvious reasons: Weltsch's essay, unsurprisingly, endorses the speaker's take on assimilationism, treating it as a fine example of "Jewish psychological interpretation" that hasn't quite found its way to Zionism. Yet the review in the liberal daily the *Prager Tagblatt* is almost as positive. Here an anonymous writer suggests that for all the wit and rhetorical artistry that went into the lecture, the speaker relied on such things less than usual, and thus managed to bring forth a persuasive "confessional statement."[6] The only problem—and Weltsch's essay, too, raises this objection—is that the speaker ended up advocating just the kind of humanist cosmopolitanism he himself dismissed as one of the "foreign ideals" that assimilationists, at their peril, have adopted.

In short, both reviewers were enthusiastic and intrigued, if also somewhat bemused. Knowing little about the speaker, and coming equipped with very different perspectives, they offered similar assessments, assessments much like Max Brod's.[7] A year earlier, Brod had ultimately disagreed with the hard-to-categorize speaker, but had nevertheless written about him, "May the cry of this outsider be heard."[8] It seems safe to say that if Weltsch and the reviewer for the *Prager Tag-blatt* had had enough time and space, they would have gone further into the speaker's background. They would have asked: just who was he? And what had led to his flashes of insight? How had he arrived at his iconoclastic, rhetorically inspired, seemingly contradictory answer to the Jewish Question?

II

Anton Kuh was born in 1890, in Vienna, to assimilated Jewish parents. He died in exile, fifty-one years later. His death is thought to have about it a bit of dark comedy, even to have been something like a final act of irony. As the story goes, Kuh was on his way to the German-Jewish Club of New York, to give a lecture titled "How I Will Survive Hitler," when he collapsed on the sidewalk, the victim of a heart attack.[9] The truth is less literary; Kuh presented his talk about Hitler in March of 1940, his heart stopped working ten months later. At the time, Kuh had been gathering materials for an autobiographical project. But, unfortunately, his notes and his collection of papers were destroyed when a wrecking ball demolished the building in which friends had stored them, and anyone looking to track Kuh's career as a critic, a feuilletonist, and a verbal performer must work around a scarcity of sources. Indeed, only a few pieces of his correspondence have survived. No one, moreover, has been able to locate a single recording of Kuh lecturing, even though he gave dozens of performances between 1917 and 1940, and his "talks" were occasionally broadcast over the radio.

On the other hand, there is a wealth of eyewitness testimony. Kuh was, if nothing else, a colorful figure, and people who met or saw or befriended him often felt moved to describe him in writing. Franz Kafka, Franz Werfel, Paul Markus,

Alfred Kerr, Berthold Viertel, Fred Hildenbrandt, Max Reinhardt, and Count Harry Kessler all penned accounts of Kuh. Some of these are very short, to be sure. Still, together with reviews, newspaper notices, and the stenographic typescript of the lecture "Zarathustra's Ape" (1925), this portraiture makes it possible to reconstruct, in considerable detail, what Kuh's performances were like. But the impressions left by contemporaries do more than that as well. They indicate that in the private sphere, too, Kuh was a theatrical and comedic presence. They also reinforce Kuh's own suggestions about the extent to which he lived by the nonconformist, antibourgeois principles he advances in his work.

For one thing, Kuh was, more or less, openly gay. For another, he was determined to avoid acquiring property and the respectability that went along with it. He spent much of his adult life residing in hotels, often as a penurious, nonpaying guest whose talents the proprietor admired. Even within his circles of bohemians and coffee house literati in Vienna and Berlin, Kuh was known as the one who was forever broke—and this despite the fact that his career went well. After all, Kuh was a prolific and highly regarded journalist, who produced well over a thousand essays and articles, and he was also a successful showman. It seemed to his friends, however, that he should have been even more successful, at least with respect to income. Kuh alternately delighted and galled them by giving away, in effect, a lot of his best material during late-night conversations. Witness the mix of admiration and lamentation in Werfel's sketch:

> Kuh was the best improviser I've ever seen. With his intoxicating squander-lust, he would bring forth, in a single night, hundreds of lethal formulations, irresistible analyses, unfettering witticisms, and real insights. After each one of these nights, he was cleaned out, like Timon of Athens; and Kuh never got anything back. It was his great riches that made him into a beggar.[10]

Some of Kuh's friends took the step of exhorting him to write down the stuff, but to no avail. When one of them went further, and hired a secretary to transcribe his spontaneous performances, so that he might earn more from his wit, Kuh simply got up and left.[11] Not that he was a kind of purist. Kuh managed to enlist the help of Imre Békessey, the Rupert Murdoch of early twentieth-century Vienna, in his campaign against Karl Kraus. But this, too, turned out to be economically disadvantageous. Having worked to escalate the feud, Kuh delivered a searing philippic against Kraus: the "Zarathustra's Ape" lecture of 1925. Kraus sued for defamation, and, in 1926, he won. Unwilling to pay the 150 schillings Kraus was awarded, Kuh left Vienna to avoid further legal trouble. Thus it was as a fugitive that he spent the latter part of the 1920s in Berlin.[12]

For all its vitriol, Kuh's attack on Kraus contains moments in which Kuh acknowledges Kraus's gifts. In one of those moments, Kuh stresses that Kraus owed his famous talent for unmasking and exposing cant to a culturally specific situation: critically observing, as a youth, "his own Jewish family."[13] It may well be that Kuh would have applied the same thinking to himself, for Kuh's family counted among its members the very type of Jewish assimilationists whom he so vigorously excoriated. There was, for instance, Kuh's grandfather, David Kuh. He founded both the Free German Party in Bohemia and the Prague-based newspaper the *Tagesbote aus Böhmen*, which he used in his efforts as a "pioneer of *Deutschtum*." And in the 1860s and 1870s, David Kuh played a key part in revealing the "Königinhofer Manuscript" to be a forgery—this meant defending the superiority of German culture, since the discovery of the manuscript was touted as the Czech answer to the Germanic sagas. It was a philological battle he fought, quite literally, until the very end. When David Kuh died, the dispute over the manuscript was ongoing, and one of Kuh's uncles eagerly took his father's place in it. Kuh's own father, Emil Kuh, was less program-matic in his support of *Deutschtum*. Yet unlike David Kuh, Emil Kuh appears to have raised his children without religious education (Anton had almost no formal knowledge of Judaism, as some of his critics pointed out). What David and Emil clearly shared was journalistic success. Having moved to Vienna early in his career, the younger Kuh wrote for, and eventually became an editor at, the liberal-centrist daily the *Neue Wiener Tagblatt*.[14]

But even if scrutinizing his family's Jewish self-fashioning helped Kuh hone his critical skills, it took a while for Jewish assimilationism to become an important theme in his writings. It also took a while, as one would expect, for Kuh's mature critical voice to emerge. At the very beginning of his journalistic career, Kuh produced feuilletons that suggest a keen interest in sexual manners and politics, but that ultimately read as conventional instances of the genre. This body of *Jugendwerk* includes "The Summer Lush" (1913), a musing on how Viennese men behave on the street when their wives are away at vacation resorts, and "Wedekind" (1914), a gushy appreciation of the playwright and his understanding of human nature. Discharged from military service because of his tic, Kuh kept operating in a straightforwardly feuilletonistic mode during the first years of the war. But by the conflict's midpoint, Kuh's thinking and writing had begun to shift, moving in the direction of greater political engagement and theoretical ambition. To a significant extent, this change was the result of his encounter with Otto Gross, an anarchist, psychological theorist, and radical critic of patriarchy, who was, as well, the father of Kuh's infant niece, Sophie.

Kuh himself once limned the course of Gross's life: "Son of a jurist, lecturer, anarchist, ship's doctor, marriage, declaration of mental unfitness, suspicion of poisoning, insane asylum, writer, rehabilitation facility, death."[15] This, obviously, is only part of the story. Born in 1877, Gross early on developed a passion for psychiatry, psychoanalysis, and drugs. His first detoxification effort occurred in 1902, at the Burghölzi clinic in Switzerland. In 1908, Gross again sought treatment for addiction to opium, morphine, and cocaine. He went back to the Burghölzi clinic, bringing with him this time well-worked-out views on mental disorders, and a bad reputation that was about to become worse. By then a self-proclaimed "sexual immoralist," Gross had, more or less simultaneously, impregnated his wife and his wife's married friend Else Jaffé-von Richthofen, with whose married sister he was also having an affair. When the children were born, both were given the name Peter, perhaps to encourage the "illegitimate" son to feel less so. The really staining thing, however, was that Gross was thought to have facilitated the 1906 suicide of the anarchist Lotte Chattmer—hence the "suspicion of poisoning" in Kuh's sketch.

All of this helped set the stage for a clash of wills and perspectives, because when Gross returned to the Burghölzi clinic, its director was none other than Carl Jung, and Jung regarded Gross's treatment as a high-profile challenge in which he simply had to succeed. But from the start, Gross resisted his efforts, using his therapy sessions as a forum for articulating his own theories, according to which neurotics should be taught precisely sexual immorality, and psychoanalysis should be used to promote a Nietzschean overturning of the dominant moral values. Jung pushed back, and eventually Gross put an end to their arguments by escaping over a wall. It would prove to be a costly solution. Incensed, Jung pronounced a diagnosis that would haunt Gross: "dementia praecox," which meant, in effect, that Gross had been deemed incurable.

Now more than ever, Gross was seen as a lunatic and a danger to society. It didn't help that Gross promptly took up with known anarchists, in both Germany and Switzerland, and soon became implicated again in a death by poisoning, namely, the 1910 suicide of the painter (and anarchist) Sophie Benz. Yet Gross continued to try to win acceptance for his theories. In the fall of 1908, for example, he published a report in *The Future*, Maximilian Harden's widely read political weekly.[16] Under the title "Parental Violence," Gross uses a harsh episode—parents committing their rebellious young daughter to a mental institution—to relate his understanding of the purpose of psychoanalysis: to defuse the repressed conflicts between "the personal and the alien." These, according to Gross, attend every normal "upbringing," because as it is normally practiced, upbringing involves exerting outside pressures against personal development.

Meanwhile, Gross's own drama of Oedipal revolt was playing out. His father was an expert on Habsburg penal and criminal law, and a man of decidedly conservative sensibilities. Having had a long career as an examining magistrate, Hans Gross spent the fin-de-siècle years as a law professor at the University of Graz. There he worked alongside—and sometimes with—the pioneering theorist of perversions Richard von Krafft-Ebing. Of the two, it was Gross who had the less liberal attitude toward sexual deviants.[17] Indeed, in an article titled "Degeneration and Deportation" (1905), the elder Gross worries about the risks society takes upon itself when it acts to save its perverse and perverted elements, and he ultimately counsels that such people should be sent away, perhaps to Southwestern Africa or the Pacific Islands.[18] Otto Gross's whole life, then, can be read as a rejection of his father's values. Moreover, Gross attacked his father in print. Or more precisely, in his book *Psychopathological Inferiorities* (1909) Gross sets about refuting his father's "Degeneration and Deportation" essay, enlisting in his effort Nietzsche's idea of "ennoblement through degeneration," whereby social progress comes through nothing other than moral deviance.[19]

Until 1913, Hans Gross refrained from striking back, and generally did what he could to support his son. More than once, in fact, he used his connections to help his son get the best treatment for his various addictions and his depression. But in the fall of 1913, Hans Gross abruptly changed tactics. Now he wielded his influence to have his son arrested in Berlin. Surprised by agents at Franz Jung's apartment, Otto Gross was brought back to Austria, where he was declared mentally unfit and put in an insane asylum against his will.

At the time, Gross had just become part of the circle of expressionist writers around Franz Pfemfert's journal *Action*, which was starting to publish his writings—writings in which Gross gives full-throated voice to his newly evolved critique of patriarchy. The conflict between "sexual morality" and "everything" that is "real and of value" had become, for him, "irresolvable." Thus only through a revolution will we find our way to "individual freedom."[20] According to Gross, this revolution will have to be unlike all previous ones, all of which have failed. It will have to have as its aim the overturning of patriarchy, for "we now recognize" that, "as the still-binding patriarchal rights in the family show, the coupling of sexuality and authority" is what "places all individuality in chains."[21] In the essay from which I have been quoting, "On Overcoming the Crisis of Culture" (1913), Gross goes on to posit, "Today's revolutionary, who, with the help of the psychology of the unconscious, can imagine relations between the sexes in a free and happy future, struggles against rape in its original form, against the father and patriarchy. The coming revolution is for matriarchy."[22] And in "Remarks on a New Ethics" (1913), which appeared in *Action* a few weeks later, Gross exhorts his readers to begin their storming of sexual morality. He tells them to campaign for sexual transgression, especially homosexuality, while again condemning marriage as rape and enslavement.[23]

So by having his son committed in such a heavy-handed manner, Hans Gross appeared to be undertaking counterrevolutionary measures, and, in a way, to be vindicating his son's thought. The father seemed to be enacting the son's assertions about the nature of patriarchal authority. A spectacular casualty of the very mechanisms he purported to have figured out, Otto Gross became a rallying point among a group of expressionists who had regarded themselves as fighting against, among other things, the soul-squashing bourgeois values of their fathers. Johannes R. Becher, Ludwig Rubiner, Jakob von Hoddis, and Else Lasker-Schüler wasted no time in publicly decrying Gross's incarceration.

When, a few years later, Kuh met Gross, the latter was thus a walking symbol of generational revolt, and he had the aura that went with that. Gross also had an aspect of genuineness that left an impression on many people, including Kafka. Recalling the night he spent on a train, in the summer of 1917, listening to Gross subject the story of Genesis to an antipatriarchal critique, Kafka noted later that there was "something authentic" about him.[24] Kuh felt the same way; utterly taken with his sister's boyfriend, he wanted to be around Gross—Kuh was present, in fact, during the long train ride with Kafka. And in order to stay close to Gross, Kuh did one of the most drastic things a Viennese intellectual could do: he switched cafés. Having been a regular at the old-world Café Central, where he had sat at Peter Altenberg's table, Kuh relocated to the more modern Herrenhof. To be sure, other factors played a role in this defection. The move was, as Kuh described it, a group phenomenon. While the "sensitive conservatives" remained loyal to the Central, its "avant-garde" patrons left (around 1918) to join the expressionist scene at the Herrenhof: Paul Kornfeld, Franz Blei, and Franz Werfel, then in his "neo-Christian anarchist" phase, were spending much of their time there. Kuh got to know all those writers. It is Gross, however, and his revolutionary, Nietzsche-inflected brand of psychoanalysis that had by far the greatest impact on him; it is Gross's work that Kuh would go on to cite repeatedly. Kuh may also have found inspiration in Gross's antic

style. At the Herrenhof, Kuh would watch closely as "the genius Gross" would "jump out of his seat every two minutes,
grab some man or woman, and take him or her with him on
his peripatetic hopping rounds through the café." Under "no
other circumstances," apparently, could Gross "pursue his
thoughts down to their last implication."[25]

On the eve of the war, Kuh was a provocative young critic
already interested in Europe's sex problems. Had Gross become his de facto brother-in-law then, well, who knows?[26]
Perhaps Kuh would have warmed to Gross and his ideas. Yet
it is hard to imagine Kuh, that "last coffee house *Literat*," as
Werfel called him, making Gross into something like his
lodestar without the context of war. Even before Kuh began to
integrate Gross's tenets into his writings, this context had
prompted him to consider the destructive workings of conventional values. Kuh was especially appalled by the mindset
that led German Jews to rush into battle when antisemitism
in Germany and Austria seemed to be on the rise. What came
to be known as the *Judenzählung* (Jewish census), for example, wouldn't have escaped Kuh's attention. Moved by the suspicion that Jews were dodging military duty, the Prussian
Ministry of War ordered a "counting up" of all the Jews in the
army. This was in 1916, and for some Jews, the effect was
alienating in the extreme. Arnold Zweig wrote to his friend
Martin Buber, "If the army were free of antisemitism, the un-
bearable call to serve would be almost easy. But to be subjected to such corrupt and vicious people! I now see myself as
a captured civilian and a stateless foreigner."[27] Kuh would ar-
ticulate similar sentiments, though he didn't confine them to
letters or the Zionist newspapers that printed some of his
writings—despite his anti-Zionism.[28] According to Max Brod,
Kuh scandalized the Jewish literary salons of Prague and Vienna during the war. In settings where "uttering the word
'Jew' had been frowned upon," Kuh made the Jewish Question a central theme. Not only that, he said "the most damn-

ing things" about the "official *Deutschtum*" of German Jews, and the "most wicked things" about "assimilated Jews" in general.[29]

Indeed, Kuh's article "Pogrom" (1918) issues a critique of assimilation that lays groundwork for the lecture he gave at the Urania House in 1919. The essay begins with the line, "A large book has remained unwritten during this war: about the tragedy of the Jews, a Samson among other nations, who turns foreign mills, always grinding for the philistines with bowed heads, blind to themselves and their fate." Kuh eventually conjectures that if the Jews press on with their assimilationism, the resistance to which it leads will only sharpen, and their fate will be awful: "In the end, an ax blow will lop off their bowed heads."[30]

And yet Kuh didn't enter the postwar period with a doom-and-gloom outlook. Energized by his critical mission, he began to garner much more notice as a public speaker, and not only did the messages he spread tend to include some uplift, but they also went, in their analyses of culture, far beyond feuilletonistic observations. Hence the feeling that Kuh had now arrived, that he had reinvented himself in the face of new challenges and possibilities. In the words of one of his contemporaries, "It was during the revolutionary moment that Anton Kuh's star rose."[31] This may seem more surprising than it should. After all, the artists and intellectuals who experienced the ferment of fin-de-siècle Vienna, and then wound up in Vienna after the war, are routinely described as having been wracked by nostalgia. In 2009, to cite just one example, the critic Nicholas Fraser sweepingly contended that the "Viennese intellectuals" who had thrived at the turn of the century "refused to accept the death of their cherished way of life." He even attributed such denial to Robert Musil. According to Fraser, Musil's *The Man without Qualities* (1931) is "an account of the empire's dying days spun out over more than a thousand pages, as if time could thus be halted and reversed."[32] But whatever we make of the novel's bulk, certainly it matters that its content satirizes the Austria of 1913, often quite bitingly. That this tone is therefore hard to miss says something about how entrenched preconceptions like Fraser's can be. Doesn't the very name that Musil gives to the old empire, "Kakania," resonate with a German slang term for excrement?

Of course, some authors did grieve over the loss of Habsburg rule, while making the new Austria out to be a scene of diminishment. Consider Stefan Zweig's characterization, in his (often-cited) memoir *The World of Yesterday* (1944): "From a logical standpoint, the most foolish thing I could have done after the collapse of the German and Austrian armies was return to Austria—to an Austria that sat on the map of Europe as a vague, gray, and lifeless shadow of the imperial monarchy."[33] But Zweig's book soon qualifies this image. The old capital, we learn, was actually becoming *too* lively for his taste, which he himself presents as being far from the norm. Indeed, Zweig complains of feeling hopelessly out of place in Vienna during an "era of the wildest experimenting."[34] He also laments that expressionism, or as he dubs it, "excessionism," had become all the rage.[35] By contrast, Kuh celebrated the arrival of expressionism after the war as "the storm from Prague that blew away the Viennese mood breezes."[36]

Often overshadowed by Weimar Germany, which has gotten far more attention from scholars, interwar Vienna was formidably innovative in its own right.[37] "Red Vienna" abounded with artists and intellectuals working creatively to act as serious agents of social reform. It was very much in keeping with the moment, for example, that Ludwig Wittgenstein signed up to become a provincial school teacher and compiled a dictionary for children. Alfred Adler took psychoanalysis to the streets, setting up free clinics for workers who wanted the treatment but couldn't afford it. Similarly inspired by the new atmosphere, Adolf Loos helped design massive public housing units. Robert Musil helped plan the restructuring of the military. Anton Webern organized workers choirs and orchestras, which he guided through performances of avant-garde compositions. Hugo Bettauer founded *He and She*, a weekly in which he agitated for "erotic liberation" by debunking traditional values and institutions—especially marriage—while integrating the nascent science of sexology into the advice columns. Though short-lived and highly controversial, the newspaper was also a tremendous hit: *He and She* quickly attracted around 200,000 readers, or about a tenth of the city's population.

Then there was the expressionist circle to which Kuh belonged. Expressionists in Vienna, as elsewhere, made up a diverse group, which was far from being uniformly radical. With Gross and Werfel, Kuh formed a coterie, and it was far more revolutionary in its hopes and dithyrambic in its tone than, say, Hermann Bahr, who in 1919 packaged "Expressionismus" as a movement whose goal was overcoming the "passive" sensory habits of impressionism. Together the three writers planned a journal of subversive "politicized expressionism": the *Blätter für die Bekämpfung des Machtwillens* (Journal of the Fight against the Will for Power). With its reference to the rather straight-laced *Blätter für die Bekämpfung des Alkoholismus* (Journal of the Fight against Alcoholism), the title carried a wry note. But the name was also a sincere statement of purpose, as well as a kind of preemptive clarification.

Like many pre- and postwar writers with ties to expressionism, Gross, Werfel, and Kuh wanted to bring about a Nietzschean uprising. They wanted to break through the rule of bourgeois values, to expose their falsity and their devitalizing character, in the hope of paving the way to a fuller, more authentic mode of existence. Yet, in contrast to many other antibourgeois writers of their day, Gross, Werfel, and Kuh didn't see the assertion of an elemental will to power as a means for achieving such ends. However much they owed to Nietzsche, they made it a point to broadcast that they were critical of him, too. For the three friends, almost every form of power was a problem, and they wanted everyone to know it.

Theirs, then, would be a different expressionist politics, and this promise resonated: along with Gross's charisma, it induced Kafka to say that he would give editorial support. Having always left these things to others, Kafka declared himself ready to shoulder part of the burden of running the magazine. He never had a chance to make good on his pledge. Because of a rift between Werfel and Gross, the journal, in which Kuh was supposed to hold forth against the "doctrines of state" in Germany and Austria, didn't find its way into print. Instead Kuh wrote for a variety of publications, including the pacifist newspaper *Peace*, which is where "Pogrom" first appeared. But at least for a while—and while developing further his critique of assimilation—Kuh helped advance his friends' respective missions, especially Gross's. Kuh undertook to show that "all evil on earth stems from sexual violence" (Gross), and to promote a nearly post-rational, practically mystical cosmopolitanism, or the ideal of "world brotherhood" (Werfel). In his book *Jews and Germans* (1921), for example, Kuh asserts, "The man of the state. Or put more exactly, he is the person who has solidarity with the Ur-sin and the mentality of sexual ownership. The revolutionary: that is the son, the enemy of the family. He is the world person. He wants to atone for his inherited guilt, and he wants a future of freely chosen relationships."[38] It was here—and in this spirit of collaboration—that Kuh unveiled the term "Jewish self-hatred." Indeed, the need for the term arose as Kuh braided together his answer to the Jewish Question with his adaptations of Gross's cultural analysis and Werfel's utopian vision.

III

Actually, Kuh had several reasons for coining the concept "Jewish self-hatred" in 1921. One of them was that he wanted to clarify his position. To be sure, lucidity was never Kuh's foremost concern. In *Jews and Germans*, in fact, he apologizes to his readers for not being *less* systematic, and his use of terminology in the book can be inconsistent, to say the least. But it also seems that Kuh wanted to head off the objections that his "Tragedy of the Jews" lecture elicited. According to reviews of the lecture, we'll recall, Kuh at once repudiated and embraced the cosmopolitan humanism that Jews had long been associated with, and that other Jewish critics, like Kuh's friend Alfred Ehrenberg, had recently celebrated as a model of identity better than both nationalist assimilationism and Zionist nationalism. And in *Jews and Germans*, Kuh takes care to stress the novelty of his perspective, or what he frames as its particularly postwar character. Kuh marks the difference between his outlook and earlier ones, and he does this, in part, by calling for a new vocabulary. The "self-criticism" that has been termed "Jewish antisemitism" should have a new name, for only now can we really see self-criticism and its potential importance for what they really are—or so Kuh claims.

A change of nomenclature was also in order because of what the concept "Jewish antisemitism" had denoted. Indeed, between 1919 and 1921, Kuh apparently brooded over the meaning of "Jewish antisemitism." In the 1919 lecture, according to Felix Weltsch's review, Kuh employed the term to describe a salutary (if rough) self-censuring that would help Jews uncover and live up to their ethical essence. Just a couple of years later, the label would no longer be right for the act of resignification that Kuh had in mind to perform. As Kuh (correctly) points out, at the beginning of *Jews and Germans*, the phrase "Jewish antisemitism" had a history of being used polemically, or by "mockers," as he puts it.[39] Of course, that didn't stop him from attempting to rework the rubric's connotations in 1919. But it isn't hard to see why, in 1921, the same approach would make less sense. Kuh had altered his understanding of Jewry's plight, in large part by bringing Gross's and Werfel's thought dramatically to bear on his views, with the result that he wanted to conjure a notion of Jewish self-contempt with meanings far grander than the one he had given "Jewish antisemitism." So instead of simply trying to rehabilitate this former term, he would coin an alternative category as well. With respect to the conventional meaning of "Jewish antisemitism," he would coin, in effect, a counterconcept. As it happens, Kuh had a name for the process of cultural revaluation he was entering into: he called it "rewording."[40]

By the time he wrote *Jews and Germans*, Kuh had radicalized his take on German nationalism, and this had meant radicalizing his critiques of both assimilationism and Zionism. The book argues that the war has finally revealed the true face of German nationalism—and along with it—the extent of German antisemitism. According to Kuh, the war has shown us what German nationalism wants in the end: "getting rid of the Jews," which would have been victory's "ultimate consequence."[41] The war was nothing less than a "*Hakenkreuzzug*," a "Swastika crusade," Kuh maintains.[42] In light of this new knowledge, Jewish assimilationism seems even more misguided than it had before, and even more hazardous as a political option. Assimilationism no longer just leads to anti-Jewish hostility: it is now "the taking on of a hostile cause as one's own."[43] As an "imitation nationalism," Zionism, too, looks worse than it had.[44]

But Kuh's reckoning with Zionism hardly ends there. Like various other efforts that aim at building self-esteem among Jews—Kuh names as an example the romanticizing of Eastern Jewry—Zionism represents a *Selbstbekennen ohne Selbsterkennen*, a "self-affirming without self-recognition."[45] Zionism stands out, however, by getting directly between Jews and the path they need to take. *Jews and Germans* challenges Jews to "break out of the family" in an unfriendly world. If Jews fail to "overcome papa," and if, psychologically speaking, they remain stuck in the "parental apartment," they will end up as so many Gregor Samsas, Kuh predicts.[46] They will be "eternally pubescent," and thus fatally stunted. And in addition to its nationalism, the problem with Zionism is that it poses a threat to young Jews trying to twist free of the father. Zionism "wears a silk patriarchal cap," Kuh writes.[47] He then explains, "Zionism says yes to what should be rejected, and sees as precious what should be destroyed: family, marriage, and a vengeful God. It blindly accepts Canaan, and its message reads: come back—back into your warm room."[48] Adding one of Werfel's leitmotifs to this analysis, Kuh also faults Zionism for being "the call of the family, rather than of the world brother."[49]

This last problem is all the more serious because bringing about world brotherhood has become a "mission" of the Jews. Kuh postulates that the long history of the Diaspora has made the Jews uniquely well prepared to realize the utopian, anti-nationalist, world brotherhood ideal. It is a calling that implies another one: opposition. Or more precisely, opposition to the existing institutional order, for example, "the state" and "marriage." Hence Kuh's lionizing of the Jews, in *Jews and Germans*, as the prospective "liberators" of all humanity. Recasting the notion of *Tikkun*—that is, repairing the world—in Gross's terms, Kuh asserts that the Jews' status as "the chosen people" rests on their potential to "free the world," and thereby allow not only for world brotherhood, but also for people to "love each other without violence."[50] Here, then, the aims of achieving "sexual revolution" and transcending the "tragedy of the Jews" are interlinked. Indeed, what Kuh wants to understand as Jewish self-hatred turns out to be the mechanism for realizing both ends, and so in its Ur-setting, the concept

"Jewish self-hatred" refers to something like a messianic force that has a lot to do with sex.

In *Jews and Germans*, "Jewish self-hatred" has less flattering connotations as well. At the beginning of the book, Kuh tells his readers that the term "self-hatred" signifies the "aesthetic self-criticism" that "mockers have named Jewish antisemitism." Not one for formal definitions, he doesn't elaborate. But Kuh does go on, confusingly enough, to use the locution from which he distances himself. Soon after introducing the notion of a singular "self-hatred" among Jews, Kuh writes that the "epoch of Jewish antisemitism lasted until the moment the war began."[51] Yet it quickly becomes evident, or at least apparent, that Kuh isn't exactly abandoning his own distinction. Rather, he is reappropriating "Jewish antimsemitism." At least for the most part, "Jewish antisemitism" stands for a broad phenomenon, in which the mindset that "self-hatred" designates has a special "role," as Kuh puts it.

Kuh thus speaks of the unique "accomplishment" that a certain type of "self-hatred" has brought about "within the history of Jewish antisemitism."[52] Not only that, it is with the particular idea of the Jews' self-hatred that Kuh's hopes manifestly lie. He wants to see the *aesthetic* self-hatred of the prewar era become politicized under postwar circumstances; he wants to see it evolve into something that will engender a revolution-inspiring self-awareness. Nowhere does Kuh assign such redemptive significance to "Jewish antisemitism." The concept of the "self-hatred" of Jews has higher meanings all its own.

But if Jewish self-hatred has already "accomplished" much, if it is vastly preferable to assimilationism and Zionism, which Kuh frames as the main political-existential alternatives for Jews—if all that is so, Jewish self-hatred has also been a problem in the immediate past, even a "psychosis." As he does with most ills, Kuh tries to trace this one back to family dynamics. What he suggests is that Jewish self-hatred isn't a radical form of assimilationism, as one might be tempted to think; rather, Jewish self-hatred at once fuels and emerges from a rebellion within (and against) highly assimilated families. This, presumably, is why the "epoch of Jewish antisemitism" coincides with the moment Kuh treats as the most advanced stage of assimilation—the period of the "social democratic" dream, which ended with the war as well. The emphasis on family dynamics may also help explain why Kuh chose the uncommon term "*Selbsthaß*." Much more than "antisemitism," "*Haß*" and "hatred" match up with that favorite theme of expressionist literature, father conflicts. "Hatred," more than "antisemitism," evokes antipathy toward what is familiar: as I noted in the previous chapter, Clement Greenberg would state—in acknowledging what he called his "Jewish self-hatred"—that "hatred is as intimate a thing as love."[53] And Jewish self-hatred, as Kuh conceives of it, is nothing if not intimate. For Jewish self-hatred to have come about, he theorizes, "a recalcitrant boy had to be born" to assimilated Jewish parents, the "knowing child" of "their curse" who counsels "rejection of the father."[54]

This call to revolt against patriarchal authority is, of course, welcome: in *Jews and Germans*, Kuh presents himself as a disciple of the recently deceased Gross, whose antipatriarchal "teachings" he summarizes at length. Moreover, the kind of Jewish self-hatred at issue here—"*this* self-hatred" on the part of Jews—has another virtue, too. It helps Jews sharpen their "self-prosecuting Jewish perspective," a faculty that will prove to be of vital importance to the fulfillment of their mission.[55] But such Jewish self-hatred has already helped Jews take strides toward real self-understanding—real *Selbsterkennen*. Hence Kuh's remark about their *Selbsthaß*: its "accomplishments have been no smaller than the harm it has caused."[56]

The harm consists, in part, of encouraging obsession, as the example of Karl Kraus, the "most typical self-hater," demonstrates. According to Kuh, Kraus has an insatiable need to root out and ridicule Jewishness everywhere. He searches for "Jewish dialect in outer space," Kuh quips.[57] Kraus responded just as cheekily, dismissing the diagnosis as a heap of "Kuhmist" (*Kuh* means "cow" in German, *Mist* "dung.").[58] But the suggestion that Jewish self-hatred had blocked his aesthetic growth was, to Kraus's mind, the crowning absurdity.

In *Jews and Germans*, Kuh maintains that "the father complex of Jewry," to borrow the formulation from Kafka's famous letter of June 1921, has made for an undue self-consciousness or "un-naïveté" among Jews, and thus Jewish *Selbsthaß* has yielded *Häßlichkeit*, or rather, "ugliness" in both life and art.[59] That the German words for "hatred" and "ugly"—*Haß* and *häßlich*—are obviously related may well have added to the appeal of the former one for Kuh. Wouldn't the shared root of the terms have served to reinforce the causal link Kuh wanted to draw, especially in the ears of an audience eager to be dazzled by his verbal magic? In any case, Kraus strikes back in the drama *Literature* (1921). A send-up of Werfel's style of expressionism, *Literature* features the acolytes of its Werfel figure belittling the literary efforts of its Kraus cipher, and at one point, those acolytes shriek at the Kraus cipher, "Jewish self-hatred! All he can do is copy our Jewish dialect!"[60] So from the start, "Jewish self-hatred" has been subjected to polemics whose misleading upshot is that the concept's meaning is largely polemical. Kraus's play implies that the concept "Jewish self-hatred" functioned as a broadside, a rather crass one. Yet just before the first account of Kraus in *Jews and Germans*, Kuh relates that for all its merits, Werfel's art, too, suffers from a surfeit of self-consciousness.[61] None other than Werfel partakes of Jewish self-hatred.

At the same time, Kuh begins to intimate that self-hatred doesn't afflict only Jews. Schopenhauer, Flaubert, Baudelaire, Wilde—with its procession of "lonely," cerebral, "permanently pubescent" figures whose path to life was blocked, the whole nineteenth century was, in a sense, an "epoch of self-hatred."[62] Indeed, Kuh wants to see the famous Jewish self-hater Otto Weininger as "a Jewish Novalis."[63] Here, too, we may have a reason why Kuh opted for "self-hatred." Seldom used before Kuh's book appeared, the word "*Selbsthaß*" carried resonances of romantic longing and melancholy. Goethe once applied the term to Byron.[64] It occurs, as well, in Karl Philipp Moritz's *Anton Reiser* (1785–90), which, along with *Wilhelm Meister*, stands as a classic German *Bildungsroman*.[65] But in the end, the Jews have the worst case of life-diminishing "intellectuality."[66] Hence Kuh's claim that because Thomas Mann's novel *Buddenbrooks* (1901) treats emotions in too analytical a manner, the book is, practically speaking, a "Jewish book."[67] Are the Jews sexually satisfied?" Kuh asks. "I would wager a no," reads his answer.[68] In part, it is as a result of their unique experience of being scattered and scorned that the Jews are the ones who are so self-reflexive—so self-reflexive that they can't even begin to get the sensual satisfaction they need to feel at peace with themselves, and at home in the world. Their ever-alert critical rationality is, Kuh muses, like a "light on in the bedroom."[69]

It turns out, however, that property even more than persecution first disrupted the Jews' erotic and interpersonal experiences, sending them on the road to their Seinfeldian condition. One of the key paradoxes in Kuh's book is that the blight of the Jews' hyper-reflexivity stems, at bottom, from a Jewish materialism, or from the drive to own as an assertion of power. This drive still manifests itself, Kuh implies, in the Jews' attachment to both assimilationism and Zionism, for both involve nationalism, and nationalism is about getting behind the territorial and power claims of a particular state. Building off of—and adapting—Gross's thought, Kuh stresses that the Jews regard themselves as the inventors of marriage. According to their own narrative, they institutionalized sexual slavery and the language that goes with it: "to own a wife" and to "belong to a husband." Thus it is the Jews who feel guiltiest about the endless "evil" marriage has caused. From this it follows that the Jews are the ones who should "free the world" and revolt against "all those things that make national, social, and cultural violence possible," to cite Andreas Kilcher's apt paraphrasing.[70] Or as Kuh himself writes, in *Jews and Germans*, "The Jews boast of having been first. Let them enjoy their rank! They claim to be the founders and sanctifiers of marriage. . . . The first are the guiltiest, and the guiltiest have been chosen to redeem the world."[71]

How will the Jews' carry out their calling? Needless to say, Kuh's mode of discourse—schematic, satirical, utopian essayism—doesn't lend itself to putting forth detailed plans. But Kuh is quite clear about one thing: the role of Jewish self-hatred in the freeing of the world. The venerable guilt that, more than anything else, makes the Jews "other" represents the deepest source of their self-hatred. And the self-hatred in which this guilt expresses itself will be the means of their redemption, and thus also the "expiation" of their guilt. Potentially, at least, Jewish self-hatred can heal itself by ushering in a future in which humans relate to each other through love. Kuh writes, "The mission of the Jews is best formulated as follows. They have the task of applying to the nations, among whom they live as guests, the recognition of guilt encapsulated in that self-hatred; they have the task of applying it to those younger, tortured students of the sins against human relations, who resist their *Geist*, which has been formed through ancient tests."[72]

Unfortunately, the Jews haven't yet learned to put *that* form of their self-hatred to such use. Jewish self-hatred has done much to uncover "Jewish guilt," which is all to the good, but Jewish self-hatred has also been too subjective and too self-involved, as strange as that may sound. Coming back to Kraus, the "most typical" Jewish self-hater, Kuh even speaks of his "impressionistic self-hatred," which is too quick to "castigate the Jewish *Geist*"—if the Jewish *Geist* is part of the problem, it is part of the solution as well.[73] What needs to happen, Kuh seems to be saying, is this: the self-consciousness of self-hating Jews must become a revolutionary consciousness. Jews must make way for and embrace their deeper, world-oriented self-hatred. And here, too, Jewish self-hatred is likely to be the agent of change. Indeed, if Kuh's book *enacts* a message, it is that Jews should look back at the past epoch, and bring their special "self-prosecuting Jewish perspective" to bear on how they appropriated just that perspective. What they will come to understand is that while Jewish self-hatred has accomplished much, it can do much more. Like the lance of Achilles—a favorite figure of Theodor Lessing—it can undo the harm it has caused. Except that when activated properly, Jewish self-hatred won't just heal what has been damaged, it will transform and revolutionize. Kuh's equation is as follows: Jewish self-hatred turned against Jewish self-hatred should amount to a step toward world love.

Toward the end of *Jews and Germans*, Kuh brings to a close his thoughts on the redemptive potential of *Selbsthaß*. He does this by way of a climactic invocation of Nietzsche. "Climactic," because throughout the book Nietzsche's influence is palpable. While Kuh takes care to distance himself from Nietzsche's notion of the will to power, he was clearly inspired, as so many expressionist writers were, by the Nietzsche who pioneered the discourses of modern man's bad conscience, shattered nerves, and debilitating self-disdain. At the same time, Kuh may also have found inspiration in the tribute Nietzsche paid to *Haß* as one of history's great *productive* forces. How "dumb human history would be" without it, Nietzsche opines in his *On the Genealogy of Morals*.[74] But the Nietzsche whom Kuh directly apotheosizes is the self-hating German intellectual—the Nietzsche who despised German nationalism; the Nietzsche who exulted over being mistaken for an Italian; the Nietzsche who once remarked, "The best author will be the one is ashamed of being a writer," and, in Kuh's words, fashioned himself as "the anti-German."[75]

Nietzsche had models of his own to draw upon, according to Kuh. In *Jews and Germans*, Jews and Germans have in common a fruitful self-hatred: among Germans, too, "self-hatred" has been "a part of the highest intellect." This tradition apparently started with Goethe and Schopenhauer. With Nietzsche, however, German self-hatred became "creatively perfected."[76] Nietzsche even brought self-hatred to the brink of being a redemptive life practice. The "exalted tragedy," Kuh maintains, was that "Nietzsche's self-hatred had prospects between storm and harbor, but got stuck in the current of the word."[77] Yet if Nietzsche was operating within a German tradition, he was, in this, at his most Jewish, because Jews are still the most advanced self-haters. And so as Kuh concludes the section at issue, he avers that he would call Nietzsche "the Kraus of the Germans," if only such naming didn't imply a "reciprocal relationship."[78] The idea underlying the qualification seems to be that because Kraus evinces lower forms of self-hatred—all that looking for Jewish dialect in outer space—alongside the self-hatred he has perfected, he doesn't quite deserve to be cast as "the Nietzsche of the Jews."

IV

In May of 1920, Kuh gave a lecture in Berlin using the same title under which he had performed six months earlier, in Prague: "The Tragedy of the Jews." It was the content that he had changed. Apparently, Kuh was fiddling with his terms— or so the most thorough review of the Berlin event indicates. Kuh is quoted, more or less, as announcing that the war had enabled him to move beyond his own "Jewish antisemitism," and become the proudest and most enthusiastic of all Jews.[79]

Or maybe the quotation is really a misrepresentation. Maybe unlike his cousin Felix, Robert Weltsch, the reviewer, couldn't quite get his head around the idea of the term "Jewish antisemitism" referring to something positive. After all, Weltsch was a Zionist, and as we know, the phrase "Jewish antisemitism" had long been used by and against Zionists as a polemical weapon. Weltsch accepted Kuh's point that German Jews were generally benighted, and he agreed that the most scathing self-criticism was therefore in order. However, Weltsch also argued that Zionists had been aware of this from the beginning, and they had acted—and were still acting—accordingly. For terminological tricks Weltsch showed little patience. Not only does his review employ "Jewish antisemitism" in a straightforwardly pejorative way, but it also declares, "The answer to the Jewish Question won't fit into a *bon mot*."[80]

What about Kuh's readers? By attacking all sides, *Jews and Germans* offered something to everyone, and, unsurprisingly, the book won quite a bit of applause. Writing in *Self-Defense*, Max Brod appreciated Kuh's critique of assimilationism, while an article in the integrationist *Allgemeine Zeitung des Judentums* praises Kuh's critique of Zionism.[81] But to point out this trend isn't to suggest that the responses were programmatic through and through. Brod's essay engages circumspectly with Kuh's "novel" use of Gross's theories.[82] The review in the *Prager Tagblatt* finds much food for thought in Kuh's speculation: the affinities between Germans and Jews might explain why both groups attract so much loathing.[83] And in his article for *The Jew*, Martin Buber's journal, the critic Elias Hurwicz seems intrigued by the idea of a redemptive *Selbsthaß* that both "recognizes the division" in Jews and "seeks to overcome it," and that is, as well, "the best piece of *Geist*" among both Germans and Jews.[84]

As far as I can tell, none of the reviewers actually adopted Kuh's understanding of "Jewish self-hatred" (nor did Kuh himself do much to follow up on his conceptual experiment). But then, of course, there were other readers, too: later readers, as well as readers who didn't speak out right away, and some may have tried to work with the meanings Kuh gave the concept, regardless of whether or not they credited Kuh. Or at least one of them may have, namely, Lessing. As we will see, Lessing's *Jewish Self-Hatred* has a lot in common with Kuh's *Jews and Germans*—despite their different stands on Zionism—and that is probably no coincidence. For in all likelihood, Lessing read Kuh's book.

Both Robert Weltsch and Brod knew about *Jewish Self-Hatred* when it was a project-in-progress and had a provisional title that evokes the title of Kuh's Jewish Question lectures, "The Tragedy of Assimilation." Thus both Weltsch, who after the Berlin lecture solicited an essay from Kuh, and Brod would likely have thought to tell Lessing about Kuh's text, which Lessing may well have been aware of anyway. Lessing and Kuh moved in the same circles: they both wrote for the cultural pages of the *Prager Tagblatt*, and they had shared allies, like Brod. Moreover, they were, in a way, allied with each other. Like Lessing, Kuh combined an inclination to ruminate fancifully on the mechanisms of injustice with a willingness to denounce concrete instances of it. And when Lessing got himself into trouble, in 1925, by presciently sizing up Hindenburg as the "zero" behind whom a "Nero" will lurk, Kuh stuck up for Lessing in print. This may be why Lessing's Nazi assassins contacted Kuh as they tracked their target. In May of 1933, Kuh was staying at the Hotel Wilson in Prague, and he would later recollect getting a "strange call," from someone looking for a "certain Lessing." That someone and his partner soon caught up with Lessing in Marienbad, where they put two bullets in his brain.[85] But we are getting far ahead of ourselves here. What I want to do now is turn to the beginning of Lessing's story.

PART THREE

Prominence: The Making of Theodor Lessing's Book *Jewish Self-Hatred*

I've finished reading Theodor Lessing's *Philosophy as Deed*. This man would be the best case to use in a highly forceful work about the coinciding of Jewishness, greatness, and decline—a historically notable coinciding, which the other paradigmatic Jews (Lessing deals with them all himself, especially the philosophers) seldom display with such clarity, or better, with such purity.

—GERSHOM SCHOLEM

Oh, let me be mawkish for the nonce!
I am so tired of being cynical!

—VLADIMIR NABOKOV (*LOLITA*)

Could there be a sadder objection to psychoanalysis? In his autobiography *Once and Never Again* (1935), Theodor Lessing confides that his relationship with his father was marked by mutual abomination, yet Lessing also tells us that he doesn't accept the theory of the Oedipus complex. The reason he gives as to why is that he hated his mother in just "as primal a way," and just as much.[1] Lessing's explanation, in its turn, invites skepticism. After all, Lessing himself suggests

that the ill will he harbored toward his mother had something
secondary about it. He detested her, he intimates, because she
didn't protect him from his father, who was his main tormen-
tor. Thus it was his father whom Lessing dreamed of murder-
ing. It was Sigmund Lessing's neck that looked so temptingly
vulnerable when he napped after lunch, and Theodor, like everyone else in the house, had to tiptoe around and speak in
whispers.[2] In any case, Lessing's was an unhappy family that
got a head start on unhappiness.

Yet Lessing's father enjoyed a childhood and a young adult-
hood very different from those that Lessing himself suffered
through. Born in 1838, in Hanover, Sigmund didn't exactly
grow up with all the advantages you could have back then, for
he was a Jew in pre-unification, pre-emancipation Germany.
That he had plenty of good fortune was nevertheless plain to
see. Sigmund was the adored youngest child of a banker and
his wife, both of whom came from families abounding in energy and cultural curiosity. Between them, Lessing's paternal
grandparents could count the following notables among their
relatives: Heinrich Heine; Ezechial Simon, the court banker
to George III; the mathematician, politician, and banker Otto
Wilhelm Wolfskehl, who was, or would be, the father of the
poet Karl Wolfskehl; and the banker and intellectual Julius
Carl Sternheim, Carl Sternheim's future grandfather. More
important, Sigmund had talents of his own that blossomed
early.

With his light complexion, blond hair, and blue eyes, he
fit in easily at school, but his social achievements went far
beyond an integration based on looks. Sigmund got along
with his schoolmates so smoothly that friends gave him the
nickname "the foreign minister."[3] If he wasn't perched at the
very top of the class, he was, moreover, quite competent in
academics. And as a medical student at the University of
Göttingen, Sigmund excelled in other areas, too. In 1859, for
example, he won the title role in a production of Schiller's

Wallenstein. Sigmund proceeded to show so much promise on stage that the court theater in Kassel offered him a job. He declined it, opting instead for the straight path to becoming a physician, and at the precociously young age of twenty-three, Sigmund passed his exams. Having partaken of the pleasures of student life at the universities in Göttingen, Würzburg, Berlin, Prague, and Vienna, he returned to Hanover in 1862 to establish his own medical practice.

It did very well, especially in the beginning. One of Sigmund's first patients was widely known to have been chronically sick. Under Sigmund's care, this person made a full recovery, and thus the fledgling doctor gained, his son would later report, a special aura, which only increased as it led aristocrats and other eminences to seek him out. But Sigmund's life soon lost its can't-miss character. The war of 1866 proved disastrous for his father's bank; the attempts to save the bank had even worse effects. Within a few years, Sigmund's father and oldest brother were broke and in jail, and his mother had died, seemingly from the stress of it all. It now fell to Sigmund to be *the* provider in the family. It was also more or less time for him to start a family of his own. Since he was under financial pressure, and had a job that brought him more respect than remuneration—and also because he had developed a taste for living in style— economic concerns figured prominently in Sigmund's considerations when he set about looking for a bride. There was nothing unusual about this, of course. The odd thing was that as he was carrying out his plan, Sigmund's social deftness deserted him in the most extreme way. Probably the sudden change of circumstances had rattled Sigmund more than he knew. Whatever the cause, his domestic life never really recovered.[4]

Sent to Düsseldorf for a stint as a military doctor, Sigmund learned of a wealthy, quirky banker named Ahrweiler who had three daughters of marrying age. Sigmund found Antonie, the middle one, to be the most beautiful and the liveliest. He soon fell in love with her, and she, for her part, was enamored of him. If it hadn't been for a complicating factor, Sigmund would have had little difficulty figuring out whose hand to ask for. Antonie had qualities that would no doubt elicit further interest, and the third daughter, too, had obvious attractions: she was brilliant, among other things. The oldest sister, Adele, however, hadn't had such luck, and to make up for the imbalance in suitor-appeal, her father had doubled her dowry. This was an offer Sigmund felt he couldn't refuse—until he felt otherwise. With the wedding date set and the guests invited, Sigmund asked Antonie, whom he had never stopped courting, to be his wife. She accepted the proposal, and together they informed her father of their intention to marry. He managed to get them to stand down by convincing them that if they went through with it, Adele would kill herself. So while full of passion for Antonie, Sigmund became her brother-in-law.

From the start, Sigmund took his frustrations out on his family, seldom missing an opportunity to scold his new wife. Still, he resolved to make the marriage work, which meant, in part, trying to have children with Adele, who soon became pregnant with Theodor. But even then Sigmund couldn't let eighteen-year-old Antonie go, and he and she persisted in carrying on an exchange of love letters. During this same time, Sigmund, Adele, and the volatile economy of the *Gründerzeit* redistributed Adele's dowry. Having spent much of it bailing out Sigmund's relatives and buying a house, Sigmund and Adele were relieved of the rest when their bank went under. Sigmund, too, was thus in a volatile state when the really bad news came, it being that Antonie had agreed to marry a banker based in Berlin. To make matters even worse, Sigmund also learned that his father-in-law would be giving Antonie and her husband as much money as Adele and he had gotten, something Herr Ahrweiler may have been planning to do all along.

It was all too much, and Sigmund, in today's parlance, lost it. He ordered Adele to pack up and return to Düsseldorf, which, being homesick, she was happy to do. Meanwhile, he raced to Berlin, where his father-in-law and Antonie were meeting with her fiancé. After storming into the house in which they were gathered, Sigmund demanded an annulment, and then proposed yet again to Antonie, who turned the offer down. Sigmund left determined to cut his ties with the family. The problem, as he soon realized, was that abandoning his pregnant wife would cause a scandal. Furthermore, if Sigmund managed to secure a divorce, his behavior might be seen as criminal, because after only a few months of marriage, he had gone through a dowry he had no way of repaying. Sigmund could only hope that a woman he had grown to hate would take him back.

When Lessing learned of the part he had played in keeping his parents together, he concluded that his father's antipathy toward him predated his birth.[5] Lessing may have been right, but it didn't help that as a child, he was far from what his socially ambitious and fervently assimilationist father wanted in a son. Both Sigmund and Adele, who was as status-oriented as her husband, aspired to come across as "regular Germans," insofar as that was possible for acculturated Jews. Indeed, Theodor discovered that he had Jewish heritage only after he participated in some antisemitic razzing of Jews at school, and was told by another child, "You're one, too!"[6] It may be that Theodor's appearance, which always vexed his father, helped give him away. Theodor was small, and unlike Sigmund, he had dark eyes and curly dark hair. In addition, Theodor was unpopular, bad at sports, and often sick.

Perhaps even more galling, though, was that Theodor was also a terrible student, for he floundered at a school whose director had once been Sigmund's closest friend. Because of his history with Sigmund, the director made sure that Theodor got extra-draconian treatment—and this at a school that appears to have specialized in humiliating its charges. According to Lessing, one of his math teachers would have the students who could solve the day's problems mock those who couldn't, which meant, for Lessing, that he often had sat puzzling over his assignment as his classmates pointed at him and made hissing noises: "zipp, zipp!"[7] But as bad as all that was, the trials of life at home were greater. Having reserved most of his pity for himself, and having grown paranoid in response to his familial woes, Sigmund experienced his son's failings as outrages and affronts.[8] He was perpetually angry with Theodor, and always ready to thrash him for the slightest misstep. Once Sigmund pummeled Theodor so severely with a riding crop that from then on, Theodor couldn't stand up straight without feeling "shooting pains," and his posture became a little more stooped. In all likelihood, this only added to his father's umbrage, for Theodor's bearing had been one of the things that would set Sigmund off.[9]

So as a youth, Lessing was beaten down at school and especially at home. Sigmund took his bitterness out on Theodor, while also treating his only son as the cause of it. Theodor, as a result, was made to feel inferior—so much so that his looming sense of inadequacy could function as a defense mechanism: next to it, the deprecations that came from the outside seemed small. Or as Lessing's autobiography explains, "I learned to survive attacks and insults by never failing to reproach myself more thoroughly and loathe myself more drastically than anyone else could."[10] Furthermore, Sigmund and Adele more or less instructed Theodor to see his Jewish heritage as something repellent, as something to be kept "covered," to use Erving Goffman's term. Reinforced many times by Lessing's friends, by the parents of friends, and by teachers and professors as well, this lesson ingrained itself in Lessing's mind, leaving him, at least according to his own account, bewildered and anguished. In *Once and Never Again*, Lessing tells us that as a young person, he would ask himself questions to the effect of, "Can a plant disown the soil out of which it grew? Am I myself not the fruit of a people and circumstances I hate and want to wipe out? Am I not damaged, lowly, ill bred, ruined?"[11]

II

Is it any wonder that Lessing, whose self-reflexive tendencies would grow only more pronounced, became a theorist of Jewish self-hatred? Indeed, in various ways Lessing's writings encourage us to link his engagement with the theme of Jewish self-hatred to his biography. During the "Lublinski affair" of 1910—in which Lessing derided the critic Samuel Lublinski as a pompous, yet also self-abasing assimilationist Jew—Lessing confessed to Martin Buber, "I am no better than Lublinski."[12] Lessing's 1913 essay on Georg Simmel addresses at length the idea that Jewish intellectuals incline to a brutal "self-blaming," then reveals that the author has been describing himself, too. The portrait is meant to stand, as Lessing puts it, as "the soul's judgment of itself."[13] The book *Jewish Self-Hatred* also draws attention to Lessing's own self-abnegating past. Lessing acknowledges, "In his youth, the author himself went through a period of total devotion to *Deutschtum*, and total reaction against *Judentum*."[14] And as we have seen, Lessing's autobiography evokes the formation of that sensibility, labeling it, albeit just once, "Jewish self-hatred."[15]

In reckoning with what they take to be Lessing's Jewish self-hatred, as well as with his interest in the topic of Jewish self-hatred, commentators have made much of Lessing's self-understanding. They have tended to cite—and to agree with—remarks like the ones I just quoted. But in a way, some of Lessing's more prominent critics have also read his narrative of developing and overcoming Jewish self-hatred against the grain. Their counterreading starts with the fact that a "total devotion to *Deutschtum*" isn't the only attachment of importance that *Once and Again* traces back to the scenes at school and home, or to the abuse that left Lessing with a special need for affirmation, affirmation he could—and did—get early on by sounding the horn of German patriotism. The book does something similar with a *völkisch* outlook that at first radicalized Lessing's dedication to Germanic ideals, but would persist well past it. Scholars have seen this philosophical attitude as being at once a driving force behind, and an enduring expression of, Lessing's own Jewish self-hatred. But Lessing himself thought otherwise, for the most part. Indeed, he suggests in *Once and Never Again* that while his youthful philosophizing exacerbated his identity conflict, it also helped him both take pleasure in life and achieve a healthy sense of self, thereby saving him from self-destruction.[16]

Encouraged by his friend Ludwig Klages, whom he met when he had to repeat a grade at school, Lessing came to recognize that despite his academic failures, he possessed a formidable intellect, which could be a joy to use. Lessing would say about Klages, "At thirteen years old, you were my mentor, my leader, my disciple, brother, companion, and everything I needed."[17] Together the two teenagers read and dreamed expansively. One of them would blaze a path for the other; they would be like Schopenhauer and Nietzsche, or like Mozart and Beethoven. Or they would influence each other as they both produced works of world-historical consequence, just as Goethe and Schiller had.

But if Lessing's relationship with Klages had the status of a sanctuary, if it gave Lessing a refuge beyond the "two hells" of school and home, it was, as well, a good place from which to seek a larger sense of community. Both Lessing and Klages, whose father was a man focused on practical matters, felt alienated in their native surroundings. While they certainly knew how to savor the bittersweet of an isolation they ascribed to their greatness, they were also attracted to ideas that helped them to see culture as part of a national cause. They were particularly inspired by a literature that fashioned itself as a response to the crisis of the *Gründerzeit*. Here the (*völkisch*) thinking was that Germany had reached a fateful fork in the road. Nationhood had its advantages; if it galvanized the German people in the right way, the *Kaiserreich* would, with its might, lead to a glory-filled epoch. For the moment, however, unification and the economic boom it had brought about were fostering destructive forces and deleterious tendencies—for example, commercialism, materialism, intellectualism, and a modern disregard for tradition. According to the boys' favorite author, Wilhelm Jordan, who gained fame by rendering the *Nibelungenlied* into contemporary language, learning about the past would help Germany usher in a heroic future, and avoid a mediocre one, or worse. What Germans needed to do was study, celebrate, and, in the end, revive the Teutonic virtues of selfless devotion to a communal soul, bravery, and physical splendor.

Adopting this ideology brought Lessing quite a few comforts. His intellectual passions now had social meaning, even urgency. And he now had a profound, or at least a profound-seeming, justification for feeling superior to his parents, who from his standpoint embodied the basest aspects of the new Germany. There was, however, an irksome catch. Many authors of Jordan's ilk anathematized the Jews as the bearers of a culture Germany had a duty to itself to transcend. That Lessing began to see his own Jewish self-hatred as philosophically motivated, and thus as deeper than his parents' parvenu self-disdain, did little to make him feel better about his background. Klages tried to help by admonishing Lessing to "struggle against" his "inborn racial soul," but Lessing still brooded over the incompatibility between his image of himself and the visions of community that fired his imagination. In *Once and Never Again*, he recalls wondering, "How would

I survive in this Aryan world full of muscular Siegfrieds with their healthy and raw ideals of strength and blood?"[18] Lessing also remarks in his autobiography, "I considered myself the offspring of the most disgusting mercenary marriage. I hated both parents and the graves of my ancestors."[19]

This mindset of "total" aversion to *Judentum* persisted for quite a while. In one of Lessing's earliest literary works, the novel *Comedy* (1894), he operates with a classic *völkisch* constellation: Jews are associated with rapacity, trickery, capitalism, and industrialization—all of which make them a threat to Germany's general health and iconic natural resources. Driven by greed, the book's three Jewish factory owners, Cahn, Cohn, and Goldstücker, maneuver to wipe out German forests. The year after *Comedy* appeared, Lessing took the step of converting to Protestantism.

Eventually, as we know, Lessing became a Zionist, something that once led commentators to divide the story of his Jewish identity into two parts: pre-Zionist self-hatred and Zionist self-reconciliation. But this approach has long fallen out of favor. For decades now, scholars have been arguing that despite Lessing's Zionism, and despite his progressive political activities, too, such as his participation in the feminist movement and his keen, costly stands against antisemitic politics and the culture of German nationalism, Lessing's conception of modern Jewry remained essentially a form of Jewish antisemitism. Their reasoning is as follows. Even after Lessing jettisoned his German nationalism, and averred that he accepted his Jewish heritage, his sensibilities stayed *völkisch*, and these sensibilities continued to inform—and to be animated by—bigoted views about Jews and Jewishness.

According to this line of interpretation, Lessing abandoned the theoretical cornerstones he and Klages laid down as youths as little as did Klages, whose writings would resonate in the most extreme antisemitic circles. Thus like Klages, Lessing continued to subject Jews to antirational and even protofascist criticisms. Didn't Lessing pen his most scathing indictments of the effeteness of modern "intellect Jews" after he turned to Zionism, around 1900? Didn't Lessing also keep using the category "Aryan" to designate a model ethnic group?[20] So what if, in the end, he tried to claim the status of Aryan for ancient Jewry? Doesn't this effort still bespeak Lessing's troubled relationship with his Jewish identity? Wasn't Lessing trying to make Jewishness and the Jewish past palatable by reconstituting them using the standards of an ideology that was hostile to Jews?

Antisemitism eventually came between Lessing and Klages. When they were both students in Munich, Klages broke off their friendship for good with the words, "You're a pushy and repulsive Jew."[21] But the connection between the two would hardly end there. Even during their own day, questions arose as to who owed more to whom. In an attempt to set the record straight, Lessing wrote an essay in which he invokes for himself the position of the more original author.[22] He also insists there that Klages and he differ in basic ways, and he does so with a measure of justification. For one thing, Lessing was the far more self-aware of the two, and when, in 1895, Lessing joined Klages in Munich, Klages and his "neo-pagan" mentor Alfred Schuler struck him as enacting a contradiction. As Lessing would later put it, "They deified the oceanic immensity of life, but they hid themselves away behind walls and towers, in towers and behind locked doors."[23] Yet Lessing's push to distinguish himself from Klages seems mostly to have heightened the sense that Lessing felt a well-founded anxiety of influence, and it is easy to see why. Just consider the titles of their works. Lessing called one of his books *Accursed Culture: Thoughts on the Opposition between Life and Mind* (1921), and another *The Decline of the Earth through Mind* (1924). A few years later, Klages published his magnum opus under the heading *The Mind as the Enemy of the Soul* (1929). And amid substantial dissimilarities, both

The Decline of the Earth through Mind and *The Mind as the Enemy of the Soul* present modern Jewry as a people of mind, or really "Geist," who have helped cause the decline of things deeper and more authentic than mind, that is, of things like soul.

This is the sort of evidence Hans Mayer has in mind when he claims, in his widely read work *Outsiders* (1975), that we should treat Lessing as a "counter-Enlightenment" figure.[24] Lawrence Baron builds a similar case on the same sort of material in the essay "Theodor Lessing: Between Jewish Self-Hatred and Zionism" (1981), which is the portrait of Lessing cited most often in the English-speaking world.[25] Baron takes as his starting point Lessing's paradoxes, and sets as his goal showing that Lessing wasn't as paradoxical as he appears to have been. "There seem to have been two Theodor Lessings," Baron begins. These were: (1) a "self-hating Jewish writer" whose "*völkisch* critique of modern society paved the way for Nazi ideology," and (2) a "courageous Jewish professor," who "championed the causes of communism, feminism, and pacifism," who "advocated Zionism as an antidote to the Jewish self-hatred that wracked assimilated Jews," and whose "outspoken Jewish nationalism and condemnations of Nazism ultimately led to his death."[26] To be sure, Baron doesn't try to resolve all the apparent contradictions he lists. As he tracks Lessing's political evolution, he proceeds, instead, to attempt to reveal how a core of Klages-like principles kept their place in Lessing's imagination, and kept on determining his understanding of the Jewish Question.

In a sense, in fact, Baron's argument belies his subtitle. For what Baron wants to demonstrate is that Lessing's Zionism *was* at bottom a kind of Jewish self-hatred, that Lessing was a "self-hating writer" even with his "outspoken Jewish nationalism," and even when "he "advocated Zionism as an antidote to Jewish self-hatred." Lessing's avowals of Jewish pride often express, according Baron, the same desires and prejudices as his German nationalism, or the same unresolved self-contempt. As a Zionist, Lessing still thought in terms of an anti-Jewish ideology. He still worked with its criteria to assess—and assail—modern Jewry, "whose national character," he maintained, "the Diaspora has disfigured beyond recognition." Making much of this line, and also the fact that Lessing wrote it well after he had become a Zionist, Baron states, "Lessing's expectations for Zionism rested on *völkisch* assumptions about primeval Jewry. He simply transposed the venerable qualities he once had associated with the Teutons to the first Jews."[27] No matter how much Lessing's Zionism evolved, Baron goes on to assert, Lessing "refused to repudiate his earlier appraisals of European Jewry as an excessively urban, commercial, and intellectual people."[28] Baron asks, as he sums up his position, "Where does constructive self-criticism leave off and Jewish self-hatred begin?" He answers, "Lessing overstepped that line of demarcation by singling out Jews to exemplify disturbing tendencies which he believed permeated all societies."[29]

As the last word in Baron's article, this claim clearly applies to Lessing's career in its entirety, including *Jewish Self-Hatred*.[30] It isn't only genealogists of the concept "Jewish self-hatred," then, who have seen Lessing's writings about German Jewry's maladies as being largely of a piece, and as stemming from emotional and theoretical dispositions that had been formed by the turn of the century. Witness also Peter Gay, who regarded the book *Jewish Self-Hatred* as another manifestation of Lessing's longstanding Jewish self-hatred. Or more precisely, witness Gay's line that the work is "part analysis and part distasteful display of masochism."[31] There is, as well, Boris Groys's introduction to the reprint edition of Lessing's text, which appeared in 1984. Groys dwells on Lessing's career-spanning links to Klages's style of "fascist" ideology, and relies on them, more than a close reading of the book, to support the proposition that the Lessing of *Jewish Self-Hatred* is "a worse instance of Jewish self-hatred than any of his case studies."[32]

In what follows, I will be arguing, in effect, for a revision of the continuity theory, and here is why. For all its insight and learning—and for all its sensitivity to how Lessing developed as a thinker—Baron's essay fails to do justice to the dynamic role of certain tensions in Lessing's work, with the result that it misses the extent of the shifts and the discursive variety to which those tensions led. Thus, as so many accounts do, Baron's leaves us with misleading impressions of Lessing's most famous book and the concept made prominent by it: "Jewish self-hatred."

Lessing wasn't simply a supporter of progressive causes whose writings often seem incongruously close to much of the reactionary cultural pessimism of his day, like the type found in Oswald Spengler's *The Decline of the West* (1922). From the very start of his career, Lessing tended to identify with the disadvantaged and the mistreated, and he philosophized on their behalf, looking for moments of consolation, for ways in which the suffering of such people might put them in privileged intellectual and ethical positions. It took Lessing a while to do this concertedly for the Jews, but he eventually did it: indeed, he does it, above all, in *Jewish Self-Hatred*, which ultimately celebrates in Jews something quite different from the *völkisch* virtues of "primeval Jewry."

Furthermore, whether or not he was willing to disavow the cultural Zionist polemics that created a stir before the First World War, Lessing, practically speaking, distanced himself from them during the Weimar Republic. He stopped producing that sort of obloquy, for one thing. And where he undertook to profile "tragic cases" among German Jewry's assimilated literati, Lessing generally brought quite a bit of sympathy to the task. Certainly this is so in *Jewish Self-Hatred*, which, for example, describes Karl Kraus as a "beautiful and pure natural talent" who should have done more with his gifts.

By then, Lessing's Zionism had undergone a whole series of transformations. In response to the war, as Baron notes, Lessing altered his political priorities and reworked his Zionism. But not only did Lessing try to blend his Zionist principles with socialist ones, he also saw his way to becoming an adherent of the maverick Zionist faction, "Poale Zionism." According to Lessing's own definition, Poale Zionism concerned itself first and foremost with "the class question," and was wary of Zionist ethno-chauvinism. It took care to think "non-nationally," as Lessing puts it in his correspondence. Accordingly, *Jewish Self-Hatred* underlines "the author's opposition to every form of nationalism."[33] This isn't to suggest that Lessing's late Zionist utterances are free of conventional propagandizing. In *Jewish Self-Hatred*, for instance, Lessing exhorts the German-Jewish literati to "harden themselves by helping to pave the road to Jerusalem." But mostly the book is propaganda for Zionism by extension—by virtue of its critique of assimilationism. In the end, the study says relatively little about Zionism, which turns out not to be the "antidote" to Jewish self-hatred. The book begins, in fact, with a discussion whose upshot is that resettlement to Palestine won't solve the problem at issue.

On the other hand, major features of Lessing's framing of the Jewish Question did, indeed, stay in place throughout his career. Just as Baron asserts, Lessing continued, after the war, to paint bleak, unflattering pictures of modern Jewry's condition, in which, like Klages, he treats *Geist* as a danger to the vivifying faculty of soul. Consider his line: "The intellect is a parasite on the life-force." But—and this is the crucial point—Lessing was also aware of the newly dramatic tensions in his later writings, as well as of how much those writings resembled discourses whose value for his right-wing enemies had become hard to miss. And he struggled with both things, scattering qualifications throughout his Weimar-era works, while worrying about their tone. In *Europe and Asia* (1918), for example, he warns against interpreting his book as a call to forsake the intellect for irrationalism. Simply abandoning *Geist* was no way to save the earth. It would be like "pulling a sword out of a tree" and watching its "vital juices run out."[34] Moreover, in a letter dated March 6, 1923, Lessing thanks Max Brod for reading *Europe and Asia*, which he was in the process of revising (and renaming *The Decline of the Earth through Mind*); then Lessing allows about his work, "I know all this must seem terribly negative and skeptical. But I simply have to press on." Not content to leave it at that, Lessing emphasizes that he has other "inclinations," too—presumably philosophical ones: "I have, as well, many positive possibilities."[35] Soon, however, his skepticism gains control again, and Lessing doubts that he will ever be able to let go and activate the affirmative side of his philosophical self.

What I want to suggest is that *Jewish Self-Hatred* represents Lessing's moment of theoretical letting go. *Jewish Self-Hatred* is still a work by Lessing, of course. It draws on old ideas and recycles formulations that had been in his corpus for a long time, even as it registers the changes in his perspective. But within both his philosophical corpus and his body of writings on the plight of modern Jewry, the book also stands out. Lessing resolves questions—such as the all-important question of *Geist*—that in his letter to Brod he complains of "wrestling with without an end in sight." Indeed, Lessing achieves his moment of resolution using just the concept "Jewish self-hatred," which takes on redemptive connotations, much as it does in Kuh's *Jews and Germans*. In Lessing's text, however, redemption may come even more easily. It is, after all, *Jewish Self-Hatred* that often does nothing other than speak the language of self-help.

This is a study, again, that imparts to its readers insights such as these: "whoever does not love himself will be loved by no one"; "don't run from your destiny"; "love your destiny";

"follow your destiny"; "there are questions that never find a solution"—except "through a strong resolution"; and also "be whatever you are, and always try to live up to your best potential." And there is much more in the book that belongs to this pattern of rhetoric, including Lessing's remark about having been exclusively devoted to *Deutschtum*. He doesn't package the statement as a call to convert to Zionism. Nor does he cite his past as a way of trying to bring Jews back to *Judentum*: "Each person must decide about that for himself," Lessing maintains. Rather, Lessing offers his own case as an extreme instance of a problem that in some measure afflicts all Jews. "There isn't a single Jew," he declares, "who doesn't carry within himself at least the beginnings of Jewish self-hatred."[36] It follows that all Jews could use his help.

III

Lessing wrote his first substantial work about German Jewry's predicament in 1901. By that time, much had changed. Having completed a course of study in medicine, as well as a dissertation in philosophy, Lessing had begun teaching at what we would today call an experimental school. This was the *Landerziehungsheim* in Haubinda, which stressed the importance of learning activities that take place outside the classroom, and especially ones that involve nature. Lessing had needed a job: he was married now, with a child on the way, and he had recently lost his main source of financial support. Lessing's maternal grandfather, who had helped him make ends meet during his student years, died in 1899. But Lessing didn't go into teaching for the money, needless to say. It stands to reason that he sought out the land school movement as a response to having been tormented in a conventional educational setting. Lessing was, in a sense, rejecting the system that had made his life so difficult. Yet the motivations behind his career choice also went beyond the hatred he harbored for traditional German pedagogy. When Lessing decided to become a teacher at a *Landererziehungsheim*, he was acting on his philosophical principles, too, and in more ways than one.

In his dissertation (1899), Lessing examines the thought of an obscure Russian-born Jewish philosopher, Afrikan Spir, whose noncanonical understanding of how knowledge is formed serves as the basis for Lessing to develop his own critical epistemology. Here Lessing begins to advance the notion that the incongruities between the empirical world and our theorizing about it aren't simply unavoidable, they are also harmful. "Begins," because he would offer further articulations of this idea in such books as *Philosophy as Deed* (1914), *Europe and Asia, History as Giving Sense to What Is Senseless* (1919), and *Jewish Self-Hatred*.

The premise of Lessing's own theorizing is that life experiences are nonidentical and unrepeatable (hence the title of his autobiography: *Once and Never Again*). Building off of the work of the now-forgotten historian Johannes Scherr, Lessing also claimed about life experiences that they are filled with senseless suffering (hence again the title of his autobiography, which stands as both an observation and an exclamation). For Lessing, what has driven much of human mental activity, what more than anything else has fostered human consciousness itself, is our need to make sense of and justify our pain-filled, essentially senseless existence (hence the title *History as Giving Sense to What Is Senseless*). The problem is that if giving sense to what is senseless, and also imposing systems of order on what is nonidentical, can make for certain psychological comforts, doing so often has the added consequence of diminishing life experience. As Lessing's (superb) biographer Rainer Marwedel has put it, reflection, according to Lessing, disturbs "the flow of life."[37] Or, to cite Lessing himself, reflection "wounds life," thereby making our lot even worse (hence the title *Accursed Culture: Thoughts on the Opposition between Life and Mind*).[38]

But as drastic as some of Lessing's pronouncements sound, he didn't—and wouldn't—treat the consciousness brought about by suffering as uniformly bad. As a medical student, Lessing was struck by the body's ability to purify and thrive on its own wastes. Sounding a bit like Derrida reading Plato, Lessing writes, in *Once and Never Again*, of his discovery that "the poison we self-destructively produce is also the cause of all detoxification."[39] This idea helped temper Lessing's pessimism, moving him to look for instances of "crisis healing itself."[40] It also inspired him to consider how injury could yield insight, something he would do throughout his career. By the late 1890s, in fact, Lessing had begun to speak of the special intelligence of women, which he saw as resulting from the particular hardships they had to endure (such as the pain of childbirth). The cruel twist, Lessing would eventually argue, was that other hardships prevented women from making effective use of their superior intelligence—even as they sharpened it. In his view, the blights that oppressed women in the most material way—political disempowerment and economic exploitation—oppressed them spiritually as well. Lessing's socialism, to a large extent, grew out of his feminism. And for its part, Lessing's feminism gained force from his commitment to altruism. An avid reader of Schopenhauer, Lessing was moved by the teaching that there should be solidarity in suffering, that we should strive to get beyond our own inevitable pain by trying to minimize the inevitable pain of others. According to Lessing's autobiography, "The final dictum of my wisdom reads: 'reduce misery!' "[41] By helping to spare students the "hell" he had been through in school, Lessing was putting that ideal into practice, and the same can be said of his campaigning for women's rights from the 1890s on.

It was because of Lessing's feminist works that he met his first wife. The plays *The Law of Life* (1896) and *Christ and*

Venus (1897) won Lessing a reputation for being an advocate of women's causes, a reputation that would be enhanced by his foreword to the German version of Maria Bashkirtseff's diaries, which appeared 1899. Yet this didn't prevent Lessing, who would repeatedly overestimate his gift for satire, from publishing a collection of would-be comic and generally platitudinous poems about the shortcomings of women: *Weiber!* (1897). Understandably, the book upset some of Lessing's admiring readers, and the correspondence initiated by one such reader, Maria Stach von Golztheim, marked the beginning of a relationship that led to marriage a few years later, and in a way, to Zionism, too. A devoted feminist and a freethinker, Maria had no reservations about marrying a person of Jewish descent. Her aristocratic parents, however, felt otherwise about the union, over which they disinherited her. Their measure offended Lessing deeply; it prompted him, and apparently Maria as well, to embrace Zionism. For Lessing, this meant resolving both to acknowledge his Jewish heritage and concern himself with the effects of antisemitic discrimination. That his character was German remained a given. As Lessing would recall about his mindset when he became a Zionist, "Around 1900, I heard about Zionism for the first time and stumbled onto a self-emphasizing, esteem-spreading principle. It didn't make me doubt my German essence [*Wesensart*]; what seemed tasteless was *to want* to be German. I certainly had the impression that I was being marginalized and excluded."[42]

The situation Lessing describes here—the one he describes as his own, that is—stands at the center of that first significant reckoning with the Jewish Question: his profile "Ludwig Jakobowski," which appeared in the Jewish magazine *East and West*, in August of 1901. Lessing begins the piece, in fact, by flagging his personal connection to Jacobowski (Lessing's spelling of the name is unusual). Jacobowski and he hadn't met in person, Lessing allows, and now they never would, for Jacobowski had died of meningitis the previous December, at thirty-two. But Lessing makes a point of mentioning that they had sought each other out, if only unsuccessfully. We learn that not long before his death, Jacobowski attempted to find Lessing at his mother's house in Hanover—Adele Lessing had been a widow since 1896.

We also learn that "for many years" the two authors carried on an epistolary conversation, and that Jacobowski had a "hard" life, which Lessing, in his evocation of it, all but directly likens to his own story. Indeed, Lessing notes that Jacobowski grew up in Berlin without emotional nurturing, and had to deal with the pressures of poverty and antisemitism as he set about launching his literary career. Yet Jacobowski nevertheless managed to remain an altruist, or full of "fiery love for humanity." Gesturing further at the affinities between himself and his subject, Lessing adds that of the "younger generation" of literati, "only" Jacobowski "truly recognized" him and "appreciated" his work.[43]

From there, Lessing turns to Jacobowski's work, and begins to reciprocate the appreciation. This was a writer, Lessing continues to emphasize, who had every reason to fall into bitterness: he was "thoroughly abused, and for too long he carried the double burden of poverty and *Judentum*." A "thousand more gifted people would have buckled under the burden," yet Jacobowski was somehow able "to wear it as a piece of jewelry," even as "the crown of his life," despite the fact that he was "physically weak and poorly formed." To be sure, encountering "restrictions everywhere," "rejection everywhere," and "humiliation everywhere" affected Jacobowski deeply, as how could it not? He developed "brooding" tendencies, which limited him artistically. Such tendencies separated him from the "sunny" genius of his hero Goethe, just as had been the case with the writers Friedrich Hebbel and

Heinrich von Kleist. But Jacobowski's melancholy also had its productive side. His "wondrous"—and most famous—book *Werther, the Jew* (1892) "grew out of that dark ground."[44]

As Lessing reads the novella, and as other critics did, too, it imparts a warning about dangers of Jewish self-hatred. The "book preaches," according to Lessing, that when a "deep, pure person" or "noble nation" is "disrespected, kept down, and scorned as common and lowly, again and again and again, a nation can become what people have made it out to be; and as soon as a person believes that he has the nature of a slave, and is ashamed of his heritage, he is already a slave." This lesson bespeaks a "deep understanding of the psychology of modern race struggles," in Lessing's estimation. It is also one that points the way to what can "bring redemption"—namely, "some love, much joy, and recognizing and taking pride in the dignity and profound greatness of our *Judentum* and its fate." From "now on, two mighty drives animated Jacobowski's work: the demand for love of humanity and the longing for happiness," for it is in "love without conflict" and "happiness" that the "wounds of the poor, despised heart can heal themselves."

In the end, however, the healing process didn't quite work out for Jacobowski. What Lessing's essay is suggesting, then, is that redemption didn't come, even though Jacobowski did everything right. Indeed, if it was short, Jacobowski's life was also highly productive. He served as an editor for *Society*, Germany's premiere journal of literary naturalism. He dedicated time and energy to helping the fledging Association for the Defense against Antisemitism. He was one of Rudolf Steiner's closest friends and most valued interlocutors, and it is fair to say that he furthered the cause of reform pedagogy (after Jacobowski's death, Steiner returned the favor by editing two volumes of his writings). And beyond all that, Jacobowski pursued and promoted love, happiness, and Jewish self-acceptance. What blocked his path, according to Lessing, is that he was so "utterly German," as "German as Heine," or as Lessing believed himself to be. To be German and forever dismissed "as a Jew"—this left Jacobowski chronically wounded, and while his wounds may have inspired a book that will "matter to our grandchildren," they also yielded a limiting "self-irony." Thus Jacobowski ended up as "the other" of his model, the untroubled genius Goethe.[45]

The divide between Jacobowski and Goethe, Lessing wants to make clear, isn't a function of ethnic hardwiring. Not only does Lessing indicate that Kleist and Hebbel were similarly unlike Goethe, he also claims that the most German art is often made by Jews who are "mixed" enough to gain more acceptance than Jacobowski could: the future Nobel Laureate Paul Heyse is one of the examples Lessing names. Furthermore, Adolf Bartels, the antisemitic critic who argued that Jacobowski's work emblematizes the Jews' literary inferiority, doesn't know anything about literature, Lessing sharply contends. On the other hand, part of Lessing's point is that Jacobowski represents an exceptional case. Most *German* Jews don't get as much out of their talent as Jacobowski did. "Oppressed" as they are, they become that lowly form of writer: "press Jews."[46]

So here there is really no way out. No amount of "pride in *Judentum*" will make Jews immune to the effects of antisemitic discrimination and degradation, and if antisemites are targeting the best and most German of Jews, if they are targeting Jews like Jacobowski, why should anyone think that tolerance is forthcoming? Moreover, since German Jews are German in their very essence, leaving Germany would amount to exile, which, presumably, would mean more wounding and more foreshortened *Bildung*, in the sense self-realization through cultural education and expression. As does Moritz Goldstein's famous, deeply ambivalent cultural Zionist essay, "The German-Jewish Parnassus" (1912), Lessing's piece presents German Jewry as struggling with a double bind. In Germany, according to Goldstein, most Jews with something to say will wind up flattened into "press Jews." Goldstein asks, "Why are there so many Jewish journalists?" His answer reads, "A journalist is a mirror that catches the images of the day and throws them back." But if Jews tear free of German culture, a good "piece of their heart will remain hanging" on it.[47]

Lessing would eventually speak, in the noncommittal subjunctive mood, about the possibility of Jews spreading German ideas in Palestine. In an article of 1910, he muses, "If I were a political organizer, I would settle among the Jews who have reversed the course of their ancestors: where their ancestors left Asia for Europe, they are winning Asia for Europe. And in Bethlehem, I would found for Asia a German university."[48] But this was really just a thought, not a program, and it was a thought Lessing wouldn't have for some years. For the time being, there seems to be no satisfying answer to the Jewish Question. Still, if self-acceptance wouldn't solve everything, it was better than nothing. This meant, in the first place, that Jews should stick up for themselves, which is what Lessing proceeded to do.

By 1902, Lessing's devotion to reform pedagogy had taken root. He had even begun to give lectures on the value of land schools. It was a commitment he was to maintain for the rest of his life. Over the years, Lessing would pen several works on land schools; and in 1920, he and his second wife, Ada, set up an alternative school in Hanover, whose directorship Ada held until 1933. But Lessing discovered early on that there were problems in the land school movement, problems having to do with reactionary thinking and antisemitic ideology. This was part of the reason why Lessing wanted to establish his own school: it was meant to be, in effect, an alternative alternative school.

Whereas Lessing saw his mission as championing what he termed "a pedagogy of joy," some his fellow teachers appeared to believe that instruction at land schools should involve encouraging students to cultivate an abhorrence of large cities and the trappings of modern life. Thus Lessing took it upon himself, in a 1907 article on land schools, to caution that it "isn't right to sow the seeds of a cheap hatred of today's urban culture and its mores. This hatred almost always leads to a hatred of all culture, to barbarism and chauvinism."[49] When he issued his call, Lessing probably had in mind Hermann Lietz, his former boss and the founder of the *Landerziehungsheim* in Haubinda. In 1902, Lietz ordered for the school a subscription to a new magazine, *The Hammer*, whose editor was Theodor Fritsch. That Fritsch was associated with the magazine may have been all Lessing needed to know. For Fritsch was a notorious antisemite; he was the forever-fulminating author of *The Antisemites' Catechism* (1887), among other tracts. Lessing's response was to exhort the Jewish students at the school to protest, which they did, but to no avail.

Not long thereafter, Lessing discovered that Lietz had added to the school's statement of purpose a provision whereby Jewish students would be admitted only in exceptional cases, and Lessing pushed back again. This time, though, he got several of his colleagues to support him (including Gustav Wyneken, who would go on to direct the land school in Wickersdorf that Walter Benjamin attended). The resistance action sufficed to make Lietz undo the change. But Lessing had seen enough, and he was convinced that the parents of the school's Jewish students had as well. As it turned out, he was wrong. Having resigned as a matter of principle, Lessing was left scrambling for a job as the Jewish students at the land school in Haubinda stayed on.

This experience couldn't have done much to raise Lessing's opinion of his fellow German Jews. Relocating did, however, energize him. He soon took a new position at a land school in Dresden, and thus began a period of what would surely vie for record busyness if there were competitions for such things. It didn't seem to matter that Lessing's first marriage had begun falling apart in the most distracting way. Although they wouldn't divorce until 1907, Maria and Lessing had become estranged by 1904, and one of the reasons why was that she had begun having an affair with a student of his. Or perhaps this spurred Lessing on, as he himself would suggest. Lessing would speak of how a philosophical work he wrote during the estrangement was really a "wrestling match" with his wife.

Here, in any event, is a partial list of what Lessing managed to do between 1904, when he began teaching at the *Landerziehungsheim* Laubgast, and 1910, when the controversy over his anti-Lublinski polemic broke out: he gave lectures against prostitution and on "the superiority of female intellectuality," and brought together his ideas about the women's cause in his book *Wife, Woman, Lady* (1910); he published a volume of poems (1908), a monograph on "hypnosis and suggestion" (1907), and a collection of essays on "aesthetics and religion" (1908); he founded and ran Germany's first "anti-noise association" (1908), and also filled the pages of its newspaper, *The Troglodyte*, with his commentary; he took up theater criticism, at first to help pay the rent, but his interest in the subject blossomed, with the result that he wrote *Theater Souls: A Study of Stage Aesthetics and the Art of Acting* (1907); he steeped himself in phenomenology in Göttingen, with none other than Edmund Husserl as his guide (1906–07); he changed careers, becoming a *Privatdozent* in philosophy at Hanover's Technical University, and to this end, he produced *Schopenhauer, Wagner, Nietzsche* (1906) and *Studies on Axiology: Investigations of Pure Ethics and Pure Law* (1908).

Lessing was, in short, in self-reinvention mode. Indeed, it was while he was launching himself into academia that he decided to refashion himself, as he would put it, as *the* "implacable scourge of Jewish degeneration." At first, he did this by way of trying his hand at travel writing. Having gone to

Galicia in 1906, Lessing later recorded as dispatches his experience of wandering through the Jewish ghettoes, and the liberal Jewish newspaper the *Allgemeine Zeitung des Judentums* published his reports in 1909. Just as it does in our own day, back then the genre called for contrivance, and Lessing's accounts are clearly full of that. In fact, some of Lessing's contemporaries called him on his meaner exaggerations, which the antisemitic press was quick to present as the most perspicacious and reliable portraiture. But whether or not Lessing actually witnessed all the things he purported to have seen, and whether or not he really had the conversations he claimed to have had, is beside the point here. Unless Lessing was willfully trying to build false consciousness, the spiritual and physical state of poor *Ostjuden* in Galicia appalled him. Nor is there any reason to doubt the sincerity of Lessing's prognosis: change, if it comes, will require some kind of "strong, powerful force." Lessing's lack of specificity in outlining a solution may have stemmed from his feeling constrained by the anti-Zionist politics of the *Allgemeine Zeitung des Judentums*. Nevertheless, that he doesn't begin to say what the force will be makes the prospect of renewal seem unlikely.

Above all, though, Lessing was struck by a certain contrast, which he continued to emphasize when he defended his "Impressions from Galicia" against the charge that it gave credence to antisemitic ideology. Almost every time Lessing conveys how overwhelmed he is by the material experience of *Ostjuden*—from their stench and their swindling to their bodies "convulsing" in prayer—he returns to the idea that the *Ostjuden* are simultaneously a people of extreme intellectuality. "All of them," Lessing writes, "appear to me to be fantastically intelligent." Having ascribed this feature to the Jews' history of persecution, Lessing observes that "more than any other people," the Jews of Galicia "put their psychic energy into a reflexive attention." A little later, he adds, "'Inner defensiveness.' From the first moment on, this seemed to me to be the most fundamental psychological characteristic of all that I saw."[50]

Yet the intellectuality of *Ostjuden* has other sources, too, including their version of Judaism. With its "unrivaled" displays of "ecstasy" and "fervor," with its "abandon," its "animal wildness," and its "awful bellowing," the religious worship of Galician Jews might lead us to think otherwise. However, next to those of Christians, the "feelings and passions of Jews are incomparably more cerebral, inward, and intellectual," because here every soul is called upon to "fight to find expression" for its "endless, unfathomable desire and suffering." Thus even though their circumstances have pushed them into a "terrifying state of physical and moral disrepair," and even in the "dirty dealings" that they have been forced to resort to, Galician Jews still manifest a "unique intellectual aura."[51] They still leave their "stamp of intellectuality" on everything they do, and they still have, one "could almost say," a "moral air." This, for Lessing, is "admirable." But it also has its downside: sounding a popular notion about "the limits of the Jews' intellectual gift," as the Jewish classicist Theodor Gomperz put it in 1904, Lessing suggests that the special intelligence of *Ostjuden* more or less precludes genius. "Precisely because the Jews are a people of talents," he writes, "genius" won't flourish. Rather, it is "destined to go under"—in "both the group as a whole and each individual member of it!"[52]

As Lessing evokes their situation, Eastern Jews are caught in a cycle that is by turns impressive and unfortunate. Being embattled enhances their longstanding intellectuality, making them, to a man, "fantastically intelligent." But "like any degraded group," Jews have formed doubts about themselves. They regard each other without the "respect and esteem" that helps individual genius bloom.[53] Meanwhile, their "intellectual ambition" coupled with their critical acumen gives them the desire and the means to keep each other down. Here, then, Lessing was picking up on one of the key concerns of his "Ludwig Jakobowski" piece, where oppression has produced legions of press Jews, and even an outlier like Jacobowski can't ascend to the level of Goethe. Lessing was doing so in a provocatively worded way, as well as with what might be described as a high degree of pessimism. Unlike Lessing, a number of Jewish authors who worried about Jewry's creative powers—from the novelist Jakob Wassermann to the philosopher Ludwig Wittgenstein—thought that genius could be found precisely among Jews who hadn't been deracinated, and especially among Eastern Jews. And as in "Ludwig Jakobowski," in "Impressions from Galicia" Lessing doesn't have an answer for the Jewish Question he raises: how to better the inner and outer condition of *Ostjuden*? Yet it would be hard to make the case that these works betray a meaningful debt to *völkisch* thinking, even amidst all the talk of "degeneration." In both texts, the Jews' reflexive intelligence is a virtue, if also a problematic one. In neither does Lessing begin to "transpose" the qualities of Teutonic heroes onto "primeval Jewry."[54]

That would come a bit later. First, Lessing would continue to engage with the themes of Jewish intellectuality and self-degradation in the here and now. Take, for example, the work that caused a far greater stir than did "Impressions from Galicia," the send-up "Samuel Takes Stock" (1910). Given the sort of rhetoric Lessing employs—at one point he imagines scores of little Lublinskis crawling up newspaper columns like monkeys—it seems reasonable to say that he had in mind to use the piece as a way of bolstering his reputation as a particularly severe critic of Jewry's condition.[55] On the other hand, the severity of the counterattacks caught Lessing off guard: he would later refer to the piece as the "little essay" that created far more trouble for him than anything else in his oeuvre. Lessing had good reason to be surprised. After all, 1910 was a kind of heyday for literary polemics in Germany and Austria, thanks in large part to Karl Kraus, whose invectives often turn on the theme of Jewish assimilation.

It was in 1910, as it happens, that Kraus blamed Heinrich Heine for bringing about a journalistic culture where cleverness is king, and all the clever Jewish journalists therefore thrive. Today, Kraus complains in his pamphlet "Heine and the Consequences," every "Itzak Wisecrack" rhymes "high art and tea cart" with alarming ease and speed.[56] Around the same time, Kraus traced Maximilian Harden's penchant for recondite formulations to his fear of coming across as a hapless Jewish journalist. Kraus also lambasted Alfred Kerr, another eminent German-Jewish critic, as an "aesthetic schlemiel."[57] Kerr, for his part, offered the following assessment of Kraus's intricate style: "Tacky plus Talmud."[58] Moreover, Kraus's fellow Jews didn't shy away from mocking his physique—one shoulder sat a little higher than the other—in the manner of an antisemitic caricature. None of this proved terribly controversial; indeed, it wasn't until after 1945 that Kraus's campaign against Heine began to elicit widespread indignation.[59] And certainly readers of the *Schaubühne*, which published "Samuel Takes Stock," were accustomed to the most unsparing tactics—not by chance would the magazine become one of Kurt Tucholsky's preferred venues.

In a way, Lessing simply had bad luck. He irked Thomas Mann, who liked Lublinski and owed him a favor, at a time when Mann was full of frustration. Almost a decade had gone by since the publication of *Buddenbrooks*, and Mann, to his dismay, had relatively little to show for it. He was blocked, and looking to unload. Hence the fact that when Mann entered the fray on Lublinski's behalf, he went after Lessing with a virulence he never again displayed publicly, execrating Lessing as "a frightful example of the miserable Jewish race." Paradoxically, Mann's screed, which appeared in the highbrow *Literarisches Echo*, deals in the same kind of abuse that Mann—and some other critics, too—had found so untoward in Lessing's polemic. Just as Lessing devotes much space to poking fun at Lublinski's "Jewish physique," Mann ridicules

Lessing's appearance, while suggesting that his looks have something to do with his being Jewish. Mann announces that "Herr Lublinski is not a handsome man, and he is a Jew," then declares that the "dwarf" Lessing is farther still from being the "perfect embodiment of Aryan masculinity." Nor does Mann shy away from addressing the most intimate sphere. More precisely, he tauntingly adverts to the unconventional breakup of Lessing's first marriage: upon learning of Maria's affair, Lessing had encouraged her and her lover, Bruno Walter, to persist in it.[60]

Lessing gave back as good as he got—and then some, perhaps. He blasted Mann for not living up to the ideals his work seemed to promote, or for being at once bitter and sentimental, and also "secretly a moralist." According to Hermann Kurzke, one of Mann's biographers, Lessing's critique hit a nerve. "That hurt," writes Kurzke, in summing up how the line I just cited affected Mann.[61] Even more painful, no doubt, were Lessing's references to Mann's being "unmanly," possibly in an erotic way. Yet the fact that Lessing knew so much about Mann may have been one of the reasons why Mann reacted as he did to Lessing, whom he now saw as an unscrupulous opportunist. Kurzke speculates that Mann wanted to push Lessing away because during his Munich days, Lessing had spent time around Mann and his circle, and Lessing had gotten to know Mann's future wife, Katja Pringsheim, and also Mann's sister Carla, too well for comfort, given Mann's homoerotic inclinations. But, again, if this closeness helped set Mann's diatribe into motion, it also helped Lessing. More than Mann, it was Lessing who could dangle unsettling suspicions. Lessing could—and did—state with confidence, "I believe that I have an acute understanding of what Thomas Mann is. Even if I am mistaken in thinking so, I still understand him better than he does me."[62]

The problem was that for all Mann's hypocrisy in the debate, his voice still carried much more weight than Lessing's.

Thus even if Lessing managed to win the battle of words, the outcome might be bad for him; and in the end, it was Lessing who suffered more damage. With its details soon forgotten, the "Lublinski Affair" quickly came to be viewed as one in which Lessing crossed the line so egregiously that Thomas Mann felt moved, as never before, to roll up his well-tailored sleeves and put another author in his place. What this has obscured is that Lessing was actually on his way to making far harsher claims about the state of German-Jewish intellectuals.

In "Samuel Takes Stock," Lessing presents Lublinski as the very embodiment of the "intellect Jew type" who, in turn, illustrates how Jewish assimilation has gone wrong. As Lessing portrays him, Lublinski, who grew up in the humblest of circumstances, tries to use his knowledge of European culture to achieve respectability—and fails. Indeed, instead of helping him garner the social rank and approval he so desires, Lublinski's strivings yield a tragic-comic spectacle. For not only does Lublinski overdo it with the erudition, and thereby give himself away as a parvenu, he has also been unable to transcend the Talmudic traditions of the Eastern-Jewish culture in which he was raised. Thus Lublinksi's attempts to write criticism in the grand style have often made for major awkwardness: Lublinski once set out to "take stock of modernity" (hence Lessing's title). Playing up the conceit of the intellect Jew's risible contradictions, Lessing has his Lublinski figure speak German-Yiddish dialect, or *Mauscheln*, as he expatiates on the fine points of German high culture. Lublinski's body, too, gets in his way, in Lessing's account of him. Lessing's Lublinski wants to appear as a commanding presence on the cultural scene, yet in "Samuel Takes Stock," what he comes across as is a fat little "synagogling."[63]

Even more essential to Lessing's profile, though, is the idea that Lublinski has become estranged from his body, and from the body in general. In one of the essay's fictional vignettes, Lublinski has so lost himself in matters of the mind that he lifts his "literary leg" and urinates in front of Lessing, seemingly unaware of what he is doing.[64] In another scene, Lessing is trying to swaddle his daughter, and to explain how bad things will be if the baby doesn't take a nap. But Lublinski, oblivious to such corporeal matters, keeps distracting him by droning on with opinions and questions about *Buddenbrooks*, Rilke, and the author Richard Schaukel.[65] Lessing's point, as he would put it in a follow-up piece, is that "Lublinski encapsulated his soul in intellectual values." A "strict judge of his epoch," Lublinski was serious and smart.[66] Yet there was also something overly abstract, something "bloodless" and self-diminishing, about his devotion to a culture that didn't embrace him back. Perhaps that very one-sidedness was too great an obstacle to surmount, Lessing seems to be suggesting. Maybe, then, Jewish critics like Lublinski would be better off spreading German culture in the Bethlehem: it was in 1910, the year of the Lublinski debacle, that Lessing started to ruminate about Jews founding a German university there.

When Lessing returned to the theme of the Jews in German culture, a couple of years later, his tone had changed. It had become soberer, and also darker, even elegiac. No doubt the fight with Thomas Mann chastened Lessing, even if it didn't ultimately put an end to his fractious streak. But Lessing's tonal shift owed more to a calamity of a different order. In April of 1912, Lessing's nine-year-old daughter, Miriam, died in an accident. The loss was devastating, of course, all the more so because Lessing played an active part in his children's upbringing, and he had enjoyed an especially close relationship with Miriam. Now a bleak situation seemed infinitely worse. Lessing was forty, and where was he? Maria and he had split up. Having spent the better part of a decade hustling to establish himself as an academic, Lessing was basically a lecturer, a lecturer without backers in a system where you needed patrons to establish yourself. As a result, he had money troubles. None of Lessing's works—scholarly or popular intellectual—had resonated as he had hoped they would. And Lessing's reputation as a critic had recently taken a big hit. According to Marwedel, Lessing entered into a "long phase of cudgeling himself with self-reproaches, and of longing for death."[67]

Toward the beginning of this lugubrious phase, Lessing wrote the essay "Jews and Artistic Accomplishment" (1912). Here he gives new emphasis to the idea of the pity of it all. Not only have German Jews had their path to genius blocked, but they have, in their travels along alternative routes, also wasted much of their intellectual and spiritual resources.[68] The theme would find even starker expression in *Philosophy as Deed*, which stresses how the Jews' special capacity for "self-censure" and "contempt for the self" have fostered their cultural difficulties. As if to provide an example of that very capacity in action, Lessing begins the book's "Excursion on the Psychology of the Jewish Intellect" with this ominous claim: "Paul de Largarde, Heinrich Treitschke, and Houston Chamberlain have leveled, as the most notable of the so-called 'antisemites,' complaints and charges that have always seemed to me to be both just and unjust. Just, insofar as they deal with clear, indisputable facts. Unjust, insofar as the truth of a judgment says nothing about its legitimacy."[69] What the leading antisemites have said is right, in other words, they just don't have the right to say it. From there, Lessing proceeds to say quite a few things that sound very much like what those antisemites had been saying. He writes that Western Jews now appear almost constitutionally incapable of genius. These "all-too smart people," who "wager to speak about everything," have an intellect that resembles a knife—"over-sharp below, but dull higher up."[70]

What we see here is that as Lessing's outlook became grimmer, his pronouncements about the Jews' situation took on a more *völkisch* character. Identity remained a complicated matter, to be sure: Lessing continued to regard himself as fundamentally German, as well as fundamentally Jewish. Yet in *Philosophy as Deed*, he refers to the Jews' squandered "racial genius." And the nations of Western Europe are now more than unwelcoming—they comprise an "alien culture." Lessing writes the following of the situation of Western Jews:

> No one wants to be what he is. Everyone strives to get far away from himself. Everyone is diligent, industrious, and energetic, but also eaten up by the desire for power and vane ambition. And so all of them waste their talent, without home and earth, on the innumerable heteronomous goals of a *foreign* culture, a *foreign* community. Everyone tries to earn respect and esteem through important accomplishments. And it becomes clear that through this eternal giving out of oneself and outdoing of oneself in accomplishments, one's own soul—one's best soul—is destroyed.[71]

As venal as they may be, the Jews' "accomplishments" still have plenty of value. Without the Jews, Lessing insists, German culture would be a shadow of its present self. And as in "Ludwig Jakobowski," in *Philosophy as Deed*, there are German Jews who ascend to impressive heights, if not quite to the rank of genius. Or more specifically, there is the philosopher Georg Simmel, whose brilliance Lessing plays up, not without an element of self-flattery. Like Jacobowski, Simmel—an institutional outsider who concerned himself with the mental effects of modern life—is an obvious point of identification for Lessing. But most Jews succumb more readily to the soul-destroying cycle partly sketched out above. Feelings of nonacceptance exacerbate the Jews' "self-tormenting" tendencies. Hyper-alert and desperate for respect, the Jews are in no position to get it. What they have accomplished in the cultural sphere may be formidable, but as a means to a mundane end, as a manic "giving out" of themselves to a *"foreign* culture," their achievements necessarily lack the soul of which works of genius are made. Indeed, this process of achieving actively destroys Jewish souls, thereby vindicating the best-known antisemites, and leaving the "most gifted" Jewish critics, who squander their talent "writing feuilletons," with all the more reason to want to be someone other than who they are.

Yet in *Philosophy as Deed*, the Jews' much-maligned intellectuality—their *Geistigkeit*—has the potential to rise to greatness. Building on his ideas about the Jews' cultural mission, Lessing posits that the "deed of our thoughts" is the Jews' "fulfilling of Israel's historical role as mediator," which means "conquering Asia for Europe," and "especially for German culture." By doing this, Lessing seems to be suggesting, German Jews could act on their Germanness and their Jewishness. By "summoning the courage" to put Lessing's version of Zionism into practice, Jews would move beyond their "nearly insane wasting of innumerable energies," and "Jewish *Geistigkeit* would become one of the most honorable forces on earth."[72] So despite the fact that Lessing's perspective had grown less sanguine, he was, for the moment, holding out a kind of Zionist answer to what he and other Zionists saw as the problems of Jews hating and "running from" themselves.

IV

But the moment wouldn't last long. If, just before the war, Lessing tried to conjure visions of the Jews winning Asia for German culture—if, despite his longstanding interest in Eastern philosophy, he remained a German cultural chauvinist up until then—he had also been critical of Germany's political culture. The outbreak of the conflict, along with Lessing's experiences as a military doctor, quickly transformed the latter tendency: Lessing radicalized his perspective in such a way that his dream of a German-Jewish cultural conquest in the Middle East fell apart. Indeed, Lessing became something of a negative chauvinist. As he puts it in his autobiography, "quite often, we should feel ashamed to be Germans." And so Lessing expanded the scope of his antiestablishment activism.

In 1922, he started contributing essays to the *Prager Tagblatt*, many of which deliver broad indictments of German society. These include "Hindenberg," the profile of 1925 that caused an uproar in right-wing circles, and cost Lessing the (nontenured) professorship he had worked so hard to get: bowing to pressure from the right, the Technical University in Hanover removed Lessing from his post, and gave him a nonteaching position. The same year also witnessed the publication of the book *Haarmann*, in which Lessing argues that the recently executed mass-murderer Fritz Haarmann should be seen as a representative product of German culture, rather than as a deviant whose death will make everyone safer. Meanwhile, Lessing deepened and developed further his socialist commitments. He started to think of the "class question" as being the most crucial one, and he reworked his Zionism in terms of it, identifying now with the communist, antinationalist Poale Zionists.

Lessing spoke out, in fact, against what he perceived to be the "chauvinism" and *völkisch* "fanaticism" of certain other Zionists. In an open letter of 1929, he complains that such Zionists have gone too far in their demands for ethnic identification. Insisting that Jews maintain a Jewish self-consciousness at all times is too limiting, and thus asking for too much. By contrast, Lessing allows—and even announces—that he doesn't always "feel Jewish." He also questions the coherence of the category "*Volkstum*," especially the notion of it that derives from "today's nationalism."[73] Yet at the same time, it is of vital importance that "the different peoples of the world— including my people, the Jews—are able to live in accordance with their own special nature." During the 1920s,

Lessing became involved with the anti-imperialism movement, and Ghandi, not Goethe, was now his hero. But, as Ghandi preached, the world's oppressed and colonized peoples won't win self-determination through nationalism. Or as Lessing himself remarks, in the 1929 letter, "No single problem of humanity will ever be solved through nationalism, least of all the problems of nations and nationalism."[74] Thus Lessing calls for "international values," more than national loyalty.

For the Jews, however, these things can coincide, because the Jews' history has made them the bearers of "supranational values" [*übervölkischer Werte*]. Here Lessing is reaching back to a slightly earlier piece "The Fate of the Jews" (1927), in which he braids together the class question and Jewish Question. With their unrivaled history of "alienation," the Jews have been through what proletarians around the world are now enduring. This thought leads Lessing to claim that "the proletariat in all countries is nothing other than a single Jewry. A giant ghetto! It is therefore self-evident that the painful experiences of the Jews can be of use to the proletariat."[75] But for all their self-evidence, the lessons of Jewish history prove elusive. Indeed, in "The Fate of the Jews," Lessing doesn't begin to say how the example of the Jews will help the world's workers.

Instead he counsels the Jews to leave Europe for "the old Asian homeland," but he doesn't hold out much hope for the success of their resettlement project. "Practical Zionism" could well turn out to be, Lessing speculates, "the final tragic accomplishment of a people whose tragic fate is preordained."[76] From there, Lessing offers a concluding invective against Christianity. Zionism is needed, because people won't stop blaming the Jews for the ills of modern life, yet it is really Christianity that is responsible for their troubles. By deifying man, Christianity, according to Lessing, degraded "the earth." The result has been a two-thousand-year-long "chain" of humans "plundering" the earth and "destroying" it. More than anything else, Christianity brought about our "gruesome" reality, which we cover up with the "web of lies" we call "world history."[77]

Such remarks hardly count as atypical. For if the war and its aftermath had the effect of intensifying Lessing's activism and his antinationalism, they also nourished his pessimism, which increased in ways that made his work appear more *völkisch*, and thus brought the basic tensions in it to a head. Lessing, who opposed the war from the start, would remember "the days of August 1914" as his "clearest revelation about our beautiful humanist delusions. Ideals are crutches. Progress is a delusion. History: lies."[78] Not by chance was it during and after the war that Lessing wrote the books on which his reputation as a "counter-Enlightenment" figure rests: *History as Giving Sense to What Is Senseless*, *Accursed Culture*, and *The Decline of the Earth through Mind*. Nor was it by chance that in 1925, Lessing published a mostly admiring volume on Nietzsche's worldview.

No longer did Lessing gesture at the possibility that the Jews could restore honor to "Jewish *Geistigkeit*" by helping to make Asia more European and, in particular, more German. For one thing, he now brooded that Western Jewry was degenerated beyond recognition and repair; it seemed "too far gone to be saved by Zionism." And for another thing, Lessing's conception of *Geistigkeit* had changed. In "The Fate of the Jews," in fact, Lessing asserts that "there is a national soul," but "there is no 'national *Geistigkeit*.'"[79] Moreover, having decided that European *Geist* is largely responsible for "the decline of the earth," Lessing began to see the Asian way as the better one, precisely because it involves less *Geist* (especially in its Hindu manifestation, or so Lessing contended). According to Lessing's *Europe and Asia*:

> The Asian person has a different bond with nature; he lives closer to the soil and the demons of the soil, more simply and with more certainty, and because of inner affinities, he lives with more knowl-

edge of the preconscious sources that move life; he lives with more knowledge than we Europeans, who have the stiff intellectual reason of our stiff consciousness."[80]

What the Jews now have going for them is their Asian past, their inherited connection to a "pagan" worldview: from about 1918 on, Lessing insisted that the Old Testament is really a "pagan work." Unfortunately, however, most Jewish intellectuals don't try to breathe life into this inheritance. They do the opposite, Lessing writes, modifying an old complaint; they "flee into *Geist*," and thus waste their spiritual resources.

And yet Lessing held to *Geist* in a way that, say, Klages didn't. In *Europe and Asia,* he maintains about *Geist* that it undoes the wounds in the individual that "consciousness" leaves. Of course, Lessing also suggests that *Geist* causes massive further damage: the diminishment of the earth[81] But once being compared to Klages had become a source of discomfort, Lessing stated his point about the upside of *Geist* even more forcefully, and with a greater sense of unease. He laments, in *Once and Never Again*:

> People hate *Geist*, the Germans more than anyone else. They feel that it is an emergency exit for the inhibited, that it is a life-diminishing force. But they don't realize one thing. Only *Geist* is like the lance of Achilles, in that it can close and heal the wounds that it causes.[82]

Another work, which was written just after Lessing had tried to clarify his "relationship with Ludwig Klages" and just after Klages's *The Mind as the Enemy of the Soul* had appeared, pushes this paradox even further—to the point where the cycle breaks open, and a troubling form of *Geistigkeit* becomes a permanent cure for the direst of maladies. The work in question is *Jewish Self-Hatred*; the *Geistigkeit* at issue is what Lessing, in the book's climactic moments, means by the concept "Jewish self-hatred."

In *Jewish Self-Hatred*, Lessing develops other ideas as well, not all of which offer as much uplift. For example, he applies his theory of why we give sense to what is senseless to the matter of Jewish persecution, and thereby suggests that the world's animus toward the Jews won't abate anytime soon. Having mistreated the Jews, the world convinced itself that it had—and has—to do so. How, then, can the Jews combat antisemitism? Since the purpose of antisemitic ideology is to justify senseless abuse, neither model behavior on the part of Jews nor rational argumentation will work, Lessing implies. And the problem of antisemitism is, of course, no insignificant one. Indeed, Lessing wastes no time in acknowledging its gravity. The beginning of his book evokes, with a sense of dismay, the violence to which anti-Jewish sentiment has been leading.[83] Not only that, internalized antisemitism has an important role in Lessing's analysis of Jewish self-hatred, just as it does in Anton Kuh's. In one place, in fact, Lessing defines "Jewish self-hatred" as a dramatic case "of the psychology of a suffering minority." He also claims that self-hatred arises from "loving those who hate you"—that is, from *Feindesliebe*.[84]

Lessing stresses, as well, that the Jews are unique in that they try to understand their persecution by looking inward, to their own defects (in his view, this is a legacy of the prophetic tradition). Taking the point a step further, Lessing asserts that the Jews' proclivity for holding themselves responsible for their woes has left them particularly vulnerable to accepting as true the counterfactual ideologies of their tormentors. As he puts it, recycling an old adage of his, "You can call a man a dog only so many times before he starts to think of himself as a dog."[85] But more clearly than any of Lessing's earlier works, *Jewish Self-Hatred* makes the case that the Jews' capacity for self-blame turns out to be an epiphenomenon, the consequence of an underlying self-hatred. The problem at the root of Jewish "self-skewering" is the self-alienating *Über-*

intellektualismus and "ethical severity" to which, according to Lessing, "the road of culture" always leads.[86]

This is why self-hatred can afflict not only "all humanity," but also "domesticated animals" as well.[87] It is also another reason why there is so much antisemitism in the world. Without acknowledging Otto Weininger's influence, Lessing follows him in emphasizing the projective mechanisms behind hatred of the Jews. People inveigh against, and try to localize in the Jews, the very things they abhor about themselves: namely, their unhappy abstraction, which has the consequence of making the Jews especially abstract and superlatively unhappy. In Lessing's (Nietzsche-inspired) account, the Jews were once the "beautiful darlings of life"—this was before the censuring prophets got the upper hand over the psalmists.[88] But the Jews have long been more embattled than others groups, and, in turn, more self-aware, more prone to a self-judging, devitalizing *Geistigkeit*. And so it is their "psychology" that best exemplifies the dynamics of self-hatred. And so it is, too, that rather than his antisemitic effusions, Weininger's discomfort with female sensuality and the messiness of life is the truly telling symptom of his Jewish self-hatred. What really matters, for Lessing, is not so much how Weininger felt about Jews, as that Weininger "hated blood."

If all this sounds gloomy, *Jewish Self-Hatred* nevertheless stands as Lessing's most upbeat work on the Jewish Question. Witness, again, his motivational talk about "loving your destiny," "being who are," "living up to your best potential," and finding "the solution" in a "strong resolution." Furthermore, Lessing's self-help rhetoric has its theoretical counterpart in the meanings Lessing ultimately gives to—or rather, draws out of and gives *back* to—his new key term, "Jewish self-hatred."

In Lessing's book as in Kuh's, the concept signifies a problem, especially at first. Lessing deems Kraus "the most revealing instance of Jewish self-hatred," because an excess of ethical severity got in the way of Kraus's "beautiful and pure natural talent."[89] Instead of composing great life-enhancing poetry, Kraus was forever berating corrupt reporters, with the result that all he had to show for his efforts was a "mountain" of dyspeptic meta-reportage. More or less the same can be said of psychoanalysis, which, as noted before, Lessing includes in his list of manifestations of Jewish self-hatred. Psychoanalysis makes what is beautiful seem ugly, according to Lessing; it emerges from and exemplifies the Jews' tragic distance from the pleasures of the material world. But even as he makes such claims, Lessing underscores the productive power of Jewish self-hatred. He refers to the Jews' "creative self-hatred" and their "self-hatred of genius," genius being something the Jews are incapable of in Lessing's other writings on them.

Like Kuh, and likely inspired by Kuh, Lessing goes on to ask his readers to embrace the paradox of a redemption-bringing role for Jewish self-hatred. To be sure, Lessing's logic can be quite different from Kuh's (though it is similarly free-wheeling throughout *Jewish Self-Hatred*). But Lessing, too, avers that the Jews' status as the first and most evolved self-haters gives them a mission of the greatest consequence. What takes place in *Jewish Self-Hatred* is a kind of climactic shift of perspective, whereby the Jews' struggle with self-hatred, as well as the special *Geistigkeit* that at once results from and comprises their self-hatred, appear as victories, even as models with which Jews could save the world.[90]

Taking his cue, perhaps, from his own rhetoric of self-help, Lessing lets go and comes close to loving what he frames as his destiny, *Geistigkeit* and all. The hopeful proposition with which, in effect, he punctuates his book appears to work as follows. More than anyone else, the Jews have dealt with the condition of self-hatred. And while self-hatred and "the darkness of *Geist*" continue to plague them, compromising their lives and their talents, the Jews have still been able to make much of themselves.[91] They have even brought self-hatred to the level of "genius," which implies achieving a kind of mastery over it, and thus the Jews can provide the world with a crucial example.[92] Even if they haven't yet formed the self-affirming "resolution" they need to get beyond "the nationality question," the Jews can become a source—or *the* source—of healing instruction for the whole world. For in the "industrial age," the "enslaving" and attendant self-alienation of most of humanity is the world's most pressing issue: "The core of all folk pathologies has been the coerced estrangement from nature and life, the forcing of people behind walls," Lessing writes.[93]

Combining, once again, the class question and the Jewish Question, only now in a more messianic spirit, Lessing purports to have figured out the "key" to Jewish history and the "secret" meaning of the Jews' "special place in the world": these have to do with the historical coinciding of Jewish emancipation and industrialization. Never mind Lessing's own tenets about the senselessness of history. That Jewish emancipation and the age of industrialization began at the same time must mean something. And what it means, according to Lessing, is that the Jews' mission is to show the world how to manage the "sickness" now spreading rapidly over the globe with the advance of the "conveyor belt," the sickness of "alienation from life" and self-hatred brought on by the industrial "ghettoizing of two-thirds of the world's population."[94] In addition, the mechanism of management is, as intimated, *Geistigkeit*.

"Before anyone else," Lessing maintains, "the Jews had to reckon with an affliction that just now has begun to threaten all peoples. The Jews had to think through and resolve problems that came about for younger and happier peoples only later." But this wasn't only a matter of self-preservation. "The Jews didn't devise their answers only for themselves," Lessing adds. "Their answers will help all those who are afflicted. The significance of the Jews, if also their great risk, lies just in how fully they have opened themselves up to a supranational, purely intellectual challenge."

As we know, Lessing was, amid much else, a medical doctor who liked biological metaphors, and as he brings *Jewish Self-Hatred* to a close, he pushes the leitmotif of disease into the metaphorical realm. In a concluding passage, he imagines the Jews and the *intellectual* gains of their experience of self-hatred as a vaccine that could save mankind from the ravages of self-hatred. This is also, I think, a fitting last word for the final chapter of my book. After all, my aim has been to track up to Lessing the affirmative meanings of what would become his signature concept. So here is that passage from the end of Lessing's *Jewish Self-Hatred*:

> The Jewish people are currently in the position of an organism that has survived an epidemic or an infection and become immune to a poisonous sickness, which is running wild among younger peoples, and whose overcoming is just now becoming the life or death question of all the peoples of the earth.[95]

CONCLUSION

One only reads well that which one reads with some quite
personal purpose. It may be to acquire some power.
It can be out of hatred for the author.

—PAUL VALÉRY

At the beginning of this book, I noted that the concept "Jewish self-hatred" is embattled in ways that "antisemitism" isn't, even though "antisemitism," too, has a complicated history of use and abuse. More than a few critics have argued that "Jewish self-hatred" belongs in scholarly discourse as an object—not as a tool—of inquiry. Analogous claims about "antisemitism" are much harder to find.

But I don't want to suggest that calls to jettison concepts are rare. Indeed, during the past few years, the value of such heavyweights as "identity," "modernity," and "assimilation" has been vigorously doubted.[1] The difference is that whereas critics of those concepts have pursued a range of questions, issues, and concerns, critics of "Jewish self-hatred" have focused their efforts more narrowly.[2] It is a difference that stems, to some extent, from the sense that today the phrase "Jewish self-hatred" can function only as a smear. After all, if that is what you think about the phrase, then what else is there to say? As one historian put it, around a decade ago, "The term 'Jewish self-hatred' is unscholarly. It is an insult, not a useful category of analysis."[3]

In more thorough reckonings with "Jewish self-hatred," we find a similar narrowness, which is clearly linked to ideas about the concept's birth—false ideas, it turns out. For the most part, Allan Janik, in his "critique" of "Jewish self-hatred," wants to track what he sees as an essentialist, activist pattern of use, which began when the notion took shape and has dominated its history.[4] The same goes for Mick Finlay and his more recent genealogy. Thus it seems reasonable to hope that a revisionist genealogy—or more specifically, one that shows how Anton Kuh and Theodor Lessing came to give "Jewish self-hatred" affirmative and even redemptive Ur-meanings— will make for more open conversations about the concept.

As it happens, shedding light on the origins of "Jewish self-hatred" also provides us with more to talk about. Janik may have had a point when he admonished scholars of German-Jewish culture to work with "Jewish self-hatred" with greater rigor and less scorn.[5] There is, however, a more widespread problem with how scholars in that field have employed the concept, and for all Kuh's comedic bluster and fanciful theorizing, his use of "Jewish self-hatred" is well worth considering as we think about a solution.

Recall what Sander Gilman does with his key term in *Jewish Self-Hatred*, a book that won Janik's approval. Drawing on Kurt Lewin's work on the group psychological dynamics of Jewish integration, Gilman proposes that Jewish self-hatred results when Jews accept as true—and see themselves through—the "mirage" of antisemitic stereotypes.[6] According to Gilman, the concept "Jewish self-hatred" is thus (or should be) "interchangeable with 'Jewish anti-Semitism.'"[7] This is, on the one hand, a broad definition. Most well-known German Jews can be made to fit it, and, indeed, Gilman treats most of them—Ludwig Börne, Heinrich Heine, Karl Marx, and so forth—as figures who betray Jewish self-hatred in one text or another.

In a way, however, Gilman's use of "Jewish self-hatred" is also tightly circumscribed. He speaks of the concept as a "valid label for a specific kind of self-abnegation," and in his study, there is, in fact, just one sort of Jewish self-hatred. If this Jewish self-hatred manifests itself in different tones and to varying degrees of severity—Heine, obviously, was no Weininger—it has mostly negative consequences. What else we can expect of internalized antisemitism, which Gilman describes as a state of confusion, even where the minds that have done the internalizing are gifted beyond measure?[8]

But why should "hatred" refer here only to self-directed antisemitic bigotry? Why shouldn't the "hatred" in "Jewish self-hatred" refer also to an animus that played itself out more fruitfully and incisively? As we know, Shulamit Volkov has taken a bold stance on this issue. There is, to be sure, some back and forth movement in her most recent account of the topic: "Excursus on Self-Hatred and Self-Criticism" (2006). At one point, Volkov claims, "[S]elf-hating Jews seem to have proliferated especially at the beginning of the twentieth century."[9] From there, however, she proceeds to argue against the idea that we should understand Jewish self-hatred as a broad, everyday social phenomenon. What Volkov ultimately stresses is just how uncommon—and how fecund—honest-to-God self-hatred was among the German-Jewish intellectuals who interest her:

> Only rarely does one find in their writings a hatred that is truly directed inward, and even then it is miraculously transformed into a source of inspiration: a starting point for creativity on the individual level and world-reforming on the public one.[10]

Here, needless to say, Volkov's use of "Jewish self-hatred" has become restrictive, strikingly so. And not only does she appear to be insisting that what the term should designate, in the first place, metamorphosed into inspiration, but she also defines "hatred" rigidly, albeit without articulating what exactly she takes it to mean. The "more typical" mix of "shame," "disgust," and "despair" shouldn't count, according to Volkov, which is why she winds up disqualifying one of her own examples of a German Jew who evinced Jewish self-hatred: the novelist Jakob Wassermann.[11] In the end, only Kafka and Lessing pass muster as actual Jewish self-haters.

Volkov's understanding of "Jewish self-hatred" as an exceptional source of ferment is itself, moreover, an exception. More often, we encounter scholars of German-Jewish culture operating with the either/or premise: salutary self-criticism and expressions of Jewish self-hatred are from top to bottom two different things. They may resemble each other at times, but we should still be able to distinguish between them, to locate a fundamental separation.

Consider, again, the question-answer sequence with which Lawrence Baron's account of Lessing ends: "Where does constructive self-criticism leave off and Jewish self-hatred begin? Lessing overstepped that line of demarcation by singling out Jews to exemplify disturbing tendencies which he believed permeated all societies." Ironically, Lessing, as much as anyone, militates against presupposing that there is such a line. For while Lessing never fully divested himself of the stereotypes he integrated into his outlook as a youth, his running critique of Jews has its moments of originality and perspicacity. This is the reason why Volkov included him in the select group of self-haters who, in her estimation, achieved a special insightfulness when their self-hatred overcame itself. But the "higher" moments in Lessing's critique don't exist in isolation from the deprecatory attitudes and ideas that helped make Lessing a controversial figure even in his own day. In works like *Philosophy as Deed*—the book that Gershom Scholem saw as illustrating a Jewish "coinciding of greatness and decline"—Lessing moves fluidly between registers. Disdainful, but hardly platitudinous, remarks about what chasing respectability has cost German Jews flow from and back into assertions about how "the antisemites" are so "right" in their judgments about so many things.

To say that Kuh's way of working with "Jewish self-hatred" accommodates such complexity better than Gilman's or Volkov's isn't to suggest that we should embrace Kuh's speculations about how Jewish self-hatred is formed, or his thoughts about how Jewish self-hatred might save the world. That is, we don't have to accept those heady propositions in order to appreciate—and find value in—the flexibility Kuh gave his fledgling concept. In *Jews and Germans*, Kuh puts under the heading "Jewish self-hatred" Karl Kraus's rebellion against what he, Kuh, regards as the cloying and development-delaying character of bourgeois Jewish life. *This* Jewish self-hatred manifests itself in Kraus's obsessive, shrill, silly attempts to find and blast "Jewish dialect" everywhere, even in "outer space." But Kuh also attributes to Kraus a related, yet different, Jewish self-hatred, thus indicating that there are varieties or types of Jewish self-hatred.

Kraus's other Jewish self-hatred is, according to Kuh, a "productive" one: it animates a critique like Nietzsche's style of German self-censure, that "best piece" of the German "intellect"—only Kraus's self-critique is even more advanced. Hence Kuh's idea that we might think of Nietzsche as the "Kraus of the Germans." Schematic in his approach until the end, Kuh doesn't tell us which of Kraus's writings he has in mind, or which ones stem from the workings of a Jewish self-hatred that *Jews and Germans* also calls "creatively perfected." But it isn't hard to come up with a surmise, for there are, indeed, different patterns in Kraus's long reckoning with German Jewry.

There are those demolition jobs in which, with grim and evident sincerity, Kraus agrees with the main claims of such antisemites as Houston Stuart Chamberlain, and accuses the great Austrian newspapers owned by Jews of secretly letting "Jewish interests" dictate editorial policy. "The way from the reporter to the rabbi is never far," he lamented.[12] And then there is the order of analysis that inspired Kafka, Scholem, and Walter Benjamin as they pondered the Jewish Question.[13] Here, too, Kraus is scabrous and acidulous, and he often works with antisemitic stereotypes. As a result, some commentators—for example, Gilman—have seen the two strands of discourse as being of a piece: a piece whose source is Jewish self-hatred. Yet in texts like "Heine and the Consequences," Kraus debunks the very stereotypes he invokes, as a provocative way of building up his aura of being absolutely paradoxical. Not only that, he assails his fellow German-Jewish writers for doing nothing other than squandering their talent on the pursuit of social capital and, even worse, succumbing to the pressure to adopt the linguistic values of their antisemitic tormentors.

Certainly this line of critique, which shaped Kraus's vaunted style, doesn't match Gilman's definition of "Jewish self-hatred." But we will be missing something if we turn away from Kuh's conceptual challenge, and take self-hatred out of the equation, for the simple reason that hatred of a group with whom Kraus ultimately identified was a part of it, a crucial part.[14] Benjamin once remarked on the "falseness" of attempts to frame Kraus's "hatred" as another emotion, such as distorted, aggrieved "love."[15] Kraus himself kept making the same point about his detestation. He often brought up his "hatred of the Jewish press," and he boasted that the "antipathy" most antisemites felt toward "Jewish things" was "child's play" next to his.[16] In a quieter moment, Kraus offered further insight into the kind of hatred he wanted to cultivate, along with a bit of advice for anyone thinking of emulating him. "Hatred must make you productive," he wrote. "If it doesn't, it is wiser to love."[17]

Introduction

1. There are, of course, other notable differences between "Jewish self-hatred" and "antisemitism." Of the two terms, "Jewish self-hatred" is the more sensational, with its connotations of self-betrayal and even derangement. And this sensational character has moved some critics to maintain that "Jewish self-hatred" is an impossibly loaded term, or that unlike "antisemitism," "Jewish self-hatred" can't effectively function as both a popular term of opprobrium and an analytic category. It can be only the former, certain critics have held—generally, as I will show, without explaining why or trying to document their position.

2. As the previous note suggests, "Jewish self-hatred" has had more than one function. It has been—and is—used as a term of practice, or of everyday discourse, as an analytic term, and as something between the two. For this reason, among others, it is necessary to move back and forth between speaking of "Jewish self-hatred" as a concept and speaking of it as a phrase, tag, label, etc. The relationship between concepts, in the sense of organizing ideas, and the terms (or words) by which concepts are known is varied and often complex. That this is so hasn't gone unnoticed, of course. Nietzsche, for example, famously discussed the complexities of the relationship (see his essay "Über Wahrheit und Lüge im außermoralischen Sinne," 1872). Robert Musil addressed them, too. He thought that concepts, by their nature, tended to fix the relationship between "words and feelings," and he worried that the perfunctory use of concepts would exacerbate that problem. Hence his lament, "Kitsch peels the life off of concepts." See Musil, *Nachlaß zu Lebzeiten*, in *Gesammelte Werke in neun Bänden*, vol. 7, ed. Adolf Frisé (Hamburg: Rowohlt, 1978), p. 503. Still, the relationship between concepts and terms warrants further inquiry, and it is, indeed, one of the themes of this book.

In part 1, I lay out what I take to be the special challenges that the relationship poses for students of conceptual history, and, in particular, for students of the concept "Jewish self-hatred." For the moment, I want to offer a somewhat more basic clarification. When quotation marks appear around the phrase "Jewish self-hatred," and I am not quoting another author, this merely indicates that I am referring to the concept or term "Jewish self-hatred" (rather than to one of the psychological conditions or complexes that the term has been used to designate, i.e., to Jewish self-hatred). Nowhere in the book will I use quotation marks to distance myself from the concept, as some authors do.

3. I should note that Kuh didn't use the formulation "*jüdischer Selbsthaß*," the exact equivalent of which would be "Jewish self-hatred." What justifies seeing Kuh as the coiner of "Jewish self-hatred" is his explicit, oppositional juxtaposing of "*jüdischer Antisemitismus*" (Jewish antisemitism) and the novel phrasing, "*Selbsthaß*" (self-hatred) "of Jews," by which Kuh meant, at times, "the Jews' special self-hatred," a reasonable translation of which would be "Jewish self-hatred." Hence the fact that it was in response to Kuh that Kuh's fellow Viennese Karl Kraus, who had decades earlier worked with the term "Jewish antisemitism," first mentioned (and mocked) the concept "Jewish self-hatred." Hence, too, the fact that the specific notion of the Jews' "self-hating tendencies" found its way into the vocabulary of Kuh's friend Max Brod just after Kuh had gone public with his concept. Then, finally, there is the fact that when Arnold Zweig brought forth one of the earliest instances of the actual wording "*jüdischer Selbsthaß*" (Jewish self-hatred), he framed it as a rubric that had been around for a while—after all, it more or less had been. Indeed, Zweig referred to "*den sogenannten jüdischen Selbsthaß*" (so-called Jewish self-hatred). On the other hand, the aim of this book isn't to show that Kuh was the first person who ever used "self-hatred" and "Jews" in the same sentence. "*Selbsthaß*," to be sure, was still an uncommon word in Kuh's day. According to Google's ngram viewer, however, the use of the term was growing more widespread. And, in fact, Leopold Liegler's book *Karl Kraus und sein Werk* (1920) loosely refers to "*Selbsthaß*" in the context of a discussion of Kraus. Here Liegler might have been picking up on Kuh's usage, which is difficult to date precisely. For the book in which Kuh unveils "Jewish self-hatred" is based on a hotly discussed oral performance, which he gave in 1920, and which evolved out of unrecorded performances that stretch back to 1919. Certainly Liegler would have known about Kuh and his attacks on Kraus, whom he, Liegler, adulated. What is clearer is

that Liegler was picking up on, and also resisting, a remark by Kraus's friend Berthold Viertel, whose use of the term "self-hating" may have influenced Kuh, whether consciously or not. In his book, Liegler cites a (recent) statement by Viertel, in which Viertel associates Kraus with the "self-hating despair" of "the messianic prophesy." Perhaps in response to Kuh's reading of Kraus in *Jews and Germans*, Viertel soon altered his position, deemphasizing the Jewishness of Kraus's self-hatred. In his 1921 book *Karl Kraus: Ein Charakter und die Zeit*, Viertel suggests that Kraus did well to spread what Viertel describes as his "self-hatred" equally "among Jews and non-Jews." Finally, if it makes sense to say that Kuh coined the concept "Jewish self-hatred," and, as well, to translate some of his constructions as "Jewish self-hatred," we should also proceed carefully here. As I stress in part 1, terminological differences that seem small can signal large conceptual shifts, and so practitioners of conceptual history should pay close attention to them. Apropos of what I will be doing in what follows, I will discuss Kraus's usage—and, of course—Kuh's below. Brod's usage can be found in Max Brod, *Heidentum – Judentum – Christentum. Ein Bekenntnisbuch*, vol. 1 (Munich: Kurt Wolff, 1922), p. 207, Zweig's in his book of 1927, *Caliban oder Politik und Leidenschaft* (Berlin: Aufbau, 1993), p. 199. See, as well, Leopold Liegler, *Karl Kraus und sein Werk* (Vienna: Richard Lányi Verlag, 1920), p. 148, and Berthold Viertel, *Karl Kraus: Ein Charakter und die Zeit* (Dresden: Rudolf Kaemmerer, 1921), p. 60.

4. Alfred Döblin, "Zion und Europa," *Der Neue Merkur* 5, no. 5 (August 1921), p. 339.

5. Friedrich Nietzsche, *Zur Genealogie der Moral, Werke in Zwei Bänden*, vol. 2, ed. Ivo Frenzel (Munich: Hanser Verlag, 1990), p. 191.

Part One: Genealogical Imperatives

1. Stadtarchiv Hannover, Theodor Lessing *Nachlaß* 1051; letter—or really, a postcard—of April 10, 1931, to Ada and Ruth Lessing—Ada was Lessing's wife, Ruth his daughter. Unless I indicate otherwise, all translations from the German in this book are mine.

2. Cited in Anatol Schenker, *Der jüdische Verlag, 1902–1938: Zwischen Aufbruch, Blüte und Vernichtung* (Niemeyer: Tübingen, 2003), p. 389. In addition to learning much from Dr. Schenker's book, I profited from epistolary discussions with him. I am grateful to Dr. Schenker for generously sharing his research with me.

3. Cited in in *Der jüdische Verlag*, p. 397.

4. Cited in Andrea Boelke-Fabian's astute and well-researched dissertation "Das Selbst und die Anderen: Über das Dilemma der Ambilanz und die schwierige philosophische Selbstbestimmung von Deutschsein und Judesein zwischen Mythos und Projektion. Theodor Lessings Essay *Der jüdische Selbsthaß* und seine Autobiographie *Einmal und nie wieder.*" (Frankfurt am Main: Johann Wolfgang Goethe-Universität, 2003), p. 29.

5. Brod, it should be noted, wrote this statement some years after Lessing's book appeared, but in doing so he was recalling his initial response to *Jewish Self-Hatred*. See Max Brod, *Streitbares Leben: Autobiographie* (Munich: Kindler, 1960), p. 93.

6. Anonymous, *Die Stimme* (February 11, 1932), p. 5.

7. Anonymous, *Jüdische Rundschau* 36, no. 9 (February 3, 1931), p. 58.

8. Cited in Boelke-Fabian, "Das Selbst und die Anderen," p. 28.

9. See Kurt Hiller's summary of a letter from Freud in Hiller, *Köpfe und Tröpfe: Profile aus einem Viertel Jahrhundert* (Hamburg: Rowohlt, 1950), p. 308.

10. Theodor Lessing, *Der jüdische Selbsthaß* (Berlin: Der jüdische Verlag, 1930), p. 25, hereafter cited as Lessing *JSH*.

11. Dr. M. K., "Um die Seele des jüdischen Menschen," *C.V.-Zeitung* (May 1, 1931), p. 225.

12. Felix Goldmann, "Jüdischer Selbsthaß!" *Der Morgen* 7, no. 5 (December 1931), pp. 450–53.

13. Allan Janik, "Viennese Culture and the Jewish Self-Hatred Hypothesis: A Critique," in *Jews, Antisemitism, and Culture in Vienna*, ed. Ivar Oxaal et al. (London: Routledge, 1987), pp. 75–88.

14. Peter Gay, *Freud, Jews and Other Germans: Masters and Victims in Modernist Culture* (New York: Oxford University Press, 1978), p. 199

15. See W.E.B. Du Bois, *The Souls of Black Folk* (New York: Vintage, 1990), p. 13; and Isaiah Berlin, "Benjamin Disraeli, Karl Marx, and the Search for Identity," in Berlin, *Against the Current: Essays in the History of Ideas*, ed. Henry Hardy (New York: Penguin Books, 1980), p. 252–86. Needless to say, this collection of essays appeared after Gay's book had been published, but Berlin's influential essay on Disraeli and Marx was originally published in 1970—or before Gay's account of Levi first appeared in print.

16. Gay, *Freud, Jews and Other Germans*, p. 183.

17. Gay, "Hermann Levi: A Study in Service and Self-Hatred," in *Freud, Jews and Other Germans*, pp. 189–230.

18. Gay, *Freud, Jews, and Other Germans*, p. 196.

19. Jacques Le Rider, *Modernity and Crises of Identity: Culture and Society in Fin-de-Siècle Vienna*, trans. Rosemary Morris (New York: Continuum, 1991), p. 264.

20. Otto Weininger, *Sex and Character: An Investigation of Fundamental Principles*, trans. Ladislaus Löb (Bloomington: Indiana University Press, 2005), pp. 272–300.

21. Allan Janik, "The Jewish Self-Hatred Hypothesis," p. 79.

22. Allan Janik, "The Jewish Self-Hatred Hypothesis," p. 79. Janik, to be sure, isn't the only critic to see Lessing as racist. Hans Mayer did, too. See Hans Mayer's "Theodor Lessing: Ein Bericht über ein politisches Trauma," in *Der Repräsentant und der Märtyrer: Konstellationen der Literatur* (Frankfurt am Main: Suhrkamp, 1971). On p. 118, Mayer speaks of Lessing a "Zionist who reasoned like a racist." I will address such characterizations at greater length in the part of this study that tracks Lessing's intellectual development.

23. In his 1931 essay on Kraus, Benjamin cites an aphorism by Kraus in which the expression "their [the Jews'] blood" occurs—or rather, he cites the aphorism in defending Kraus against the charge that he was a Jewish antisemite. See Walter Benjamin, "Karl Kraus," in *Illuminationen*. ed. Siegfried Unseld (Frankfurt am Main: Suhrkamp, 1977), p. 364.

24. Lessing, *JSH*, p. 20.

25. Lessing, *JSH*, pp. 92–93.

26. See Susan Glenn's incisive article, "The Vogue of Jewish Self-Hatred in Post-World War II America" *Jewish Social Studies* 12, no. 3 (Spring–Summer 2006), pp. 95–137.

27. See Glenn, "The Vogue of Jewish Self-Hatred."

28. See www.masada2000.org.

29. David Mamet, *The Wicked Son: Anti-Semitism, Self-Hatred, and the Jews* (New York: Schocken, 2006) p. 10.

30. Limbaugh made the remark on his radio show in 2006. Transcript posted on www.mediamatters.org/mmtv/200608090015; accessed August 9, 2006.

31. See Barak Ravid, "Netanhayu's Paranoia Extends to 'Self-Hating Jews' David Axelrod and Rahm Emmanuel," *Haaretz* (July 9, 2009), online at http.haaretz.com/print-edition/news/netanyahu-s-paranoia -extends-to-self-hating-jews-emanuel-and-axelrod-1.279611.

32. This, of course, isn't to suggest that in the 1970s, 1980s, and 1990s, no one associated strident criticism of Israel with Jewish self-

hatred. Sander Gilman, for example, drew just such a connection. Toward the end of his well-known study of Jewish self-hatred, which appeared in 1986, he writes, "One of the more recent forms of Jewish self-hatred is the virulent Jewish opposition to the state of Israel." Gilman, *Jewish Self-Hatred: Anti-Semitism and the Hidden Language of the Jews* (Baltimore, Johns Hopkins University Press, 1986), p. 391.

33. Cited in Patricia Cohen, "Essay Linking Liberal Jews and Anti-Semitism Sparks a Furor," *New York Times* (January 31, 2007), online at http.nytimes.com/2007/01/31/arts/31jews.html?scp=6&sq=tony%20 judt%20anti-semitism&st=cse.

34. Janik, "The Jewish Self-Hatred Hypothesis," p. 81 and note 7 on p. 248.

35. Antony Lerman, "Jews Attacking Jews," *Haaretz* (September 12, 2008), online at http.haaretz.com/print-edition/opinion/jews-attacking -jews-1.253684.

36. R. C. Conard, review of *The Anti-Journalist*, published in August 2008, in *Choice Reviews* online at www.cro2.org/default.aspx?page =reviewdisplay&pid=3392352.

37. Conard, review of *The Anti-Journalist*.

38. See Paul Mendes-Flohr, *Divided Passions: Jewish Intellectuals and the Experience of Modernity* (Detroit: Wayne State University Press, 1991), pp. 67–76; Todd Endelman, "Jewish Self-Hatred in Britain and Germany," in *Two Nations: British and German Jews in Comparative Perspective*, ed. Michael Brenner et al. (Tübingen: Niemeyer, 1999), pp. 331–64; and Shulamit Volkov, "Excursus on Self-Hatred and Self-Criticism," in *Germans, Jews, and Antisemites: Trials in Emancipation* (Cambridge and New York: Cambridge University Press, 2006), pp. 33–46.

39. Mick Finlay, "Pathologizing Dissent: Zionism, Identity Politics, and the 'Self-Hating Jew,'" *British Journal of Social Psychology* 44 (2005), p. 202. Finlay applies this critique to Gilman on p. 206.

40. Gilman, *Jewish Self-Hatred*, p. 2.

41. See Finlay, "Pathologizing Dissent," p. 208; here Finlay suggests that Karl Kraus portrayed Herzl as being a "self-hating Jew," when, in fact, Kraus accused Herzl of being a "Jewish antisemite."

42. Finlay, "Pathologizing Dissent," p. 211. The term "Jewish self-hatred" appears to have been introduced, as we will see, soon after the First World War. But the term didn't achieve a measure of prominence until later, especially after the publication of Lessing's book. Google's ngram viewer shows a sharp spiking of its use around 1930. An equally sharp drop-off occurred not long thereafter, no doubt as a result of the

Nazi seizure of power and its concomitants—censorship, exile, etc. In a sense, then, the original discussion of Lessing's book and his key term was truncated. After the war, the German term *"jüdischer Selbsthaß"* remained in disuse; it didn't regain—and surpass—its former stature in Germany until the 1960s.

43. Finlay, "Pathologizing Dissent," p. 211.

44. Reinhart Koselleck, *The Practice of Conceptual History: Timing History, Spacing Concepts*, trans. by Todd Presner and Kirsten Behnke (Stanford: Stanford University Press, 2002), p. 20.

45. This isn't to suggest that the study of conceptual history in general suffers from a lack of methodological self-reflexivity. To the contrary, it is easy to name examples of recent works that meet the particular challenges of conceptual history with sophistication and insight. Two that I found especially insightful are Peter Gordon, *Continental Divide: Heidegger, Cassierer, Davos* (Cambridge: Harvard University Press, 2010), which isn't, first and foremost, a conceptual history, but contains edifying thoughts on the evolution of concepts, and Samuel Moyn, *The Last Utopia: Human Rights in History* (Cambridge: Harvard University Press, 2010).

46. According to Bendavid, a number of other obstacles stood in the way of successful Jewish emancipation and integration (which he nevertheless campaigned for). Indeed, for some Jews, integration was simply out of reach. One of the chief obstacles, as Bendavid saw it, was the entrenchment of the rabbinic tradition. A Kantian and well-known figure in the Berlin "Jewish Enlightenment," Bendavid called, in effect, for Jews to abandon what he regarded as the debilitating superstitions of the rabbis. He wanted to see Jews return to the "teachings of natural religion," which "Mosaic law" represents. But as Sven-Erik Rose has noted in his perceptive account of Bendavid's work of 1793, *Something on the Characteristics of Jews*, Bendavid was, as well, deeply concerned with the psychology, or really, the pathology, of the oppressed. And Bendavid often sounds more proto-Nietzschean than Kantian in his response to the Jewish Question. Witness this line from his book: "The first main mistake of the Jews is that of all slaves. Envy of their masters. Contempt for their fellow slaves." See Bendavid, *Etwas zur Charackteristik der Juden* (Leipzig: Josef Stabel, 1793), p. 14. See also Sven-Erik Rose, "Jewish Hydra, German *Heimat*, and the 'Jewish Question:' Judaism and Subjectivity in Lazarus Bendavid, Berthold Auerbach, and Karl Marx," Ph. D. diss., University of Pennsylvania, 2003, pp. 12–142. It is worth noting that Bendavid published in, and was also part of the circle

around, what was likely the first journal of psychology: Karl Philipp Mortiz's *Magazin zur Erfahrungsseelenkunde*. Also likely is that Bendavid's perceptions of Jewry were influenced by Solomon Maimon's rather grim account of the Eastern-Jewish community into which he was born, parts of which first appeared in the *Magazin* in 1792: Bendavid and his fellow Kantian Maimon were friends and interlocutors. In his autobiography, Maimon writes, for example, "A whole series of factors combined to obstruct the course of my development and hinder the workings of my natural aptitudes. All this was involved: the shape Poland was in back then and the condition of our people within Poland. We were like a donkey buckling under a double burden—the weight of our own ignorance and the religious prejudices that were bound up with that ignorance, and the weight of the Polish majority's ignorance and the religious prejudices that were bound up with that ignorance." Solomon Maimon, *Lebensgeschichte* (Frankfurt am Main: Jüdischer Verlag, 1995), p. 66. See also Martin Davies. "Karl Philipp Moritz's Erfahrungsseelenkunde: Its Social and Intellectual Origins," *Oxford German Studies* 16 (1985), pp. 13–35.

47. Ritchie Robertson, *The 'Jewish Question' in German Literature: Emancipation and Its Discontents, 1749–1939* (Cambridge: Cambridge University Press, 1999), p. 70.

48. By the time Lewin wrote his essay, there was, in the United States, a longstanding discussion of self-contempt among ethnic and religious minorities, and there are a few of instances of the English term "Jewish self-hatred" that predate Lewin's "Self-Hatred among Jews." These, however, come from the 1930s, and may well have been inspired by Lessing's study. For example, in a 1934 book, the novelist, translator, and student of German literature Ludwig Lewisohn writes of Marx's "Jewish self-hatred," and Lewisohn, being steeped in German letters, certainly would have known about Lessing's *Jewish Self-Hatred*. Hence, perhaps, the fact that the formulation "Jewish self-hatred" doesn't occur in the novel about Jewish self-disdain that Lewisohn wrote just before Lessing's book appeared: *The Island Within* (1928). The 1934 book I adverted to is *The Permanent Horizon: A New Search for Old Truth* (New York: Harper & Brothers, 1934). Still, it was through Lewin's essay that the term "Jewish self-hatred" began to gain prominence in the Anglo-American public sphere.

49. Cited in Robertson, *The 'Jewish Question' in German Literature*, p. 67. See also Hannah Arendt, *Rahel Varnhagen: The Life of a Jewess*, ed.

Liliane Weissberg, trans. Richard and Clara Winston (Baltimore: Johns Hopkins University Press, 1997), especially pp. 250–59.

50. See Jonathan Hess's profoundly innovative and informative study *Middlebrow Literature and the Making of German-Jewish Identity* (Stanford: Stanford University Press, 2010), which, quite frankly, alerted me to all the works of middlebrow fiction I discuss here.

51. *Förderung und Hemmniß* first appeared in *Allgemeine Zeitung des Judentums* (1841), with no name given for the author. It was reprinted in Ludwig Philippson, *Saron: Novellenbuch*, vol. 2 (Lepizig: Leopold Schauß Verlag, 1856), pp. 217–61. The line about "self-contempt" occurs on page 254.

52. Anonymous (i.e., Philippson), "Vorurtheile: Scenen aus dem Leben," *Jüdisches Volksblatt* 9 nos. 36–37 (July–September, 1862), pp. 141–43, 145–47.

53. Marcus Lehmann, *Säen und Ernten, Der Israelit* 11 nos. 25–52 (June 1– December 28, 1870), pp. 466–68, 487–88, 507–8, 526–28, 546–48, 566–68, 583–84, 602–4, 618–20, 635–36, 655–56, 671–72, 687–88, 707–8, 727–28, 747–48, 778–80, 795–96, 811–12, 827–28, 846–47, 867–68, 882–84, 898–900, 918–20, 939–40, 959–960, 965–66.

54. The phrase "Jewish antisemites" appears, for example, both as the title and in the body of a piece in the Berlin orthodox newspaper *The Jewish Press* 13 no. 52 (December 28, 1882), p. 586; the piece is a screed against a writer deemed to be a Jewish atheist. We find the formulation "Jew with antisemitic inclinations" in a critique of a reform rabbi published in an 1886 issue of *The Israelite* 27, no. 25 (March 29, 1886), p. 441. "Jewish Jew-hatred" occurs in the first supplement of *The Israelite* 42, no. 68 (August 29, 1901), pp. 1495–96.

55. Theodor Herzl, *Der Judenstaat, in Gesammelte Werke*, vol. 1. (Berlin: Der jüdische Verlag, 1934), p. 30.

56. Karl Kraus, "Eine Krone fur Zion," *Karl Kraus: Fruhe Schriften 1892–1900*, ed. J. J. Brackenburg (Munich: Kösel, 1979), p. 299.

57. Kraus, Untitled essay, *Die Fackel* 11 (Mid-July 1899), p. 6.

58. The Zionist newspaper Herzl founded, *Die Welt*, would, however, continue to employ the expression "Jewish antisemites."

59. That man has become tired of himself is, for Nietzsche, clearly a crucial problem, perhaps the crucial problem of modernity. At the same time, Nietzsche's relation to self-hatred is complex. He valorized a certain type of self-scorn, as we will see later in this chapter. And as we will see in part 3 of this book, as Nietzsche lays out the origins of modern

self-hatred in *On the Genealogy of Morals*, he suggests that the self turned against itself has, in some ways, been a powerfully productive, even indispensable force in human history.

60. Hermann Bahr, *Wien* (Stuttgart: Krabbe, 1906), p. 69.

61. Theodor Herzl, *AltNeuland* (Norderstedt: haGalil, 2004), p. 221.

62. Heinrich von Treitschke, "Unsere Aussichten," in *Der Berliner Antisemitimusstreit*, ed. Walter Boehlich (Frankfurt am Main: Insel, 1988), p. 9.

63. Emanuel Schreiber, *Die Selbstkritik der Juden* (Berlin: Duncker Verlag, 1880), p. xii.

64. Thomas Mann, "Wälsungenblut," *Schwere Stunden* (Frankfurt am Main: Fischer, 1991), p. 127. Mann wrote the story in 1905, but withdrew it when rumors began to spread that he was about to publish an antisemitic work. Thus the story first appeared, in a private edition, years later—during the Weimar Republic (or in 1921).

65. Mann, "Wälsungenblut," p. 128.

66. Arthur Schnitzler, *Der Weg ins Freie*, in *Gesammelte Werke von Arthur Schnitzler in zwei Abteilungen*, part 1, vol. 3 (Berlin: Fischer, 1912), p. 176.

67. Kurt Lewin, "Self-Hatred among the Jews," in Lewin, *Resolving Social Conflicts & Field Theory in Social Science* (Washington, D.C.: American Psychological Association, 1997), pp. 133–42.

68. Sigmund Freud, "Analyse der Phobie eines Fünjährigen," *Sigmund Freuds Gesammelte Werke, Chronologisch geordnet*, vol. 7 (Frankfurt: Fischer, 1966), p. 271.

69. Freud, "Analyse eines Fünjährigen," p. 271.

70. Cited in Max Schur, *Freud: Living and Dying* (New York, International Universities Press, 1972), p. 468.

71. See Freud, *Der Mann Moses und die Monotheistische Religion, Sigmund Freuds Gesammelte Werke, Chronologisch geordnet*, 16:103–246.

72. Cited in Gay, *Freud, Jews, and Other Germans*, p. 195.

73. Gay, *Freud, Jews, and Other Germans*, p. 197.

74. On the transmission of Fliess's theory to Weininger, see Chandak Sengoopta, *Otto Weininger, Sex, Science, and Self in Imperial Vienna* (Chicago: University of Chicago Press, 2000), p. 104 f.

75. This isn't to imply that Weininger could only, or must, have gotten his theory of bisexuality from Fliess and Freud. After all, 1900 was, if nothing else, a propitious moment for unsettling lines of demarcation that had once seemed stable. Moreover, Fliess wasn't the only one to

press on traditional thinking about sexual orientation. In Berlin, for example, Magnus Hirschfeld had begun to do that as well. The point is that, as many scholars have pointed out, Weininger was likely influenced by conversations with Swoboda that drew on what the latter had learned from Freud.

76. Weininger, *Sex and Character*, p. 12.

77. Weininger, *Sex and Character*, p. 42.

78. Weininger, *Sex and Character*, p. 275.

79. Weininger, *Sex and Character*, p. 275.

80. Fritz Wittels, *Der Taufjude* (Vienna: Breitenstein, 1904).

81. Theodor Lessing, *Einmal und nie wieder* (Gütersloh: Bertelsmann, 1969), p. 112.

82. See Lawrence Baron, "Theodor Lessing: Between Jewish Self-Hatred and Zionism," *Leo Baeck Institute Year Book* 26 (1981), pp. 323–40.

83. See Baron, "Theodor Lessing," p. 333.

84. Lessing, *Einmal*, p. 297.

85. See Binjamin Segel, *Die Entdeckungsreise des Herrn Dr. Lessing zu den Ostjuden* (Lemberg: Hatikwa, 1910).

86. The more splenetic of these writings is the essay on Lublinski, which appeared in the *Schaubühne* in 1910 and was widely condemned as having gone too far. On the Lublinski affair, see Rainer Marwedel's excellent biography of Lessing, *Theodor Lessing, 1872–1933: Eine Biographie* (Darmstadt: Luchterhand, 1987), pp. 132–43. Marwedel's treatment of Lessing's writings about Jews is generally judicious. However, Marwedel's focus lies elsewhere—and his biography contains very little commentary on Lessing's book *Jewish Self-Hatred*.

87. Lessing, *Intellekt und Selbsthaß: Eine Studie uber den judischen Geist* (Heidenheim: Antaios, 2007), p. 34. This volume is a suggestively titled republication of Lessing's 1913 essay on the philosopher Georg Simmel.

88. Lessing, *Intellekt und Selbsthaß*, p. 34.

89. Lessing, *Intellekt und Selbsthaß*, p. 46.

90. Lessing, *Intellekt und Selbsthaß*, p. 44.

91. Lessing, *Intellekt undSelbsthaß*, p. 26.

92. Lessing, *Intellekt und Selbsthaß*, p. 26.

93. Gilman, *Jewish Self-Hatred*, p. 301. For Gilman, it is worth noting, the concept "Jewish self-hatred" was originally a manifestation of the phenomenon of Jewish self-hatred. Hence the emphasis he places on the role that the notions of the "sick Jew" and "the rhetoric of race"

played in its "development." Hence, too, Gilman's investment in the idea that there is a "proto-fascist" aspect to Lessing's thinking about Jewish self-hatred. See Gilman, *Jewish Self-Hatred*, p. 302.

94. Gilman, *Jewish Self-Hatred*, p. 393.

95. Shulamit Volkov, "Excursus on Self-Hatred and Self-Criticism," p. 37.

96. Volkov, "Excursus," p. 37.

97. Using the website http.compactmemory.de, one can search a large number of (digitized) German-Jewish newspapers for individual words and phrases—newspapers that in some cases existed throughout the nineteenth century and into the twentieth. A search for such phrases as "*Selbsthaß des Judentums*" and "*jüdischer Selbsthaß*" yields no results from before the First World War and relatively few from the Weimar period. Searches using Google books produce roughly the same results. Still, and as I mentioned in an earlier note, one could fiddle with this dating. Kuh probably began to use "self-hatred" in a lecture given in 1920—again, he claimed that the 1921 book in which he coins the term is a transcription (from memory) of the lecture. Reviews of his lectures, however, tend not mention the term; they speak only of Kuh's appropriation of "Jewish antisemitism." In any case, "self-hatred," where it is "self-hatred of Jews" and clearly means "Jewish self-hatred"—and is, as well, presented as an alternative to the "misappropriated" category "Jewish antisemitism"—first occurs in Kuh's published writings in 1921. For the Weltsch quotation, see Andreas Kilcher's introduction Anton Kuh, *Juden und Deutsche*, ed. Kilcher (Vienna: Löcker, 2003), p. 43, hereafter cited as Kuh *JD*.

98. This argument represents a substantial revision of the one I advanced in an earlier article: "Zionism and the Rhetoric Jewish Self-Hatred," *The Germanic Review* 83, no. 4 (Fall 2008), pp. 343–64. There I emphasized—or rather, overemphasized—the continuities between Lessing's book on self-hatred and his turn-of-the-century writings on the Jewish Question, while suggesting that the term was born of rhetorical exigency. Rehashing old content made coming up with a new label all the more urgent—this was my explanation as to why Lessing's terminology changed in 1930, and it is close to the one Andrea Boelke-Fabian puts forth in her dissertation "Das Selbst und die Anderen," see p. 27. What Boelke-Fabian and I failed to appreciate sufficiently is that despite numerous moments of reaching back and self-citation, the self-hatred book develops a message quite foreign to Lessing's previous work. Part of the aim of the present book is to bring this shift to light.

Otherwise put, the goal here is to show that rather than making up for a lack of intellectual movement, Lessing's use of the term "Jewish self-hatred" actually corresponds to a notable shift in his message. *On the Origins of Jewish Self-Hatred* also supersedes my other earlier attempt to sketch a genealogy of "Jewish self-hatred," "Interwar Expressionism, Zionist Self-Help Writing, and the Other History of 'Jewish Self-Hatred,'" *The Leo Baeck Institute Yearbook* 55 (2010), pp. 179–93.

99. On the discourse of self-help in this context, see Michael Cowan, *The Cult of the Will: Nervousness and German Modernity* (University Park: Pennsylvania State University Press, 2008).

100. As mentioned above, I am (or was), in a way, one of those scholars; Andrea Boelke-Fabian is another. She states that the appeal of the term "Jewish self-hatred" lay largely in its being more "markant"—or pithier—than the alternatives.

101. This isn't to imply that "Jewish self-hatred" has anything like univocally positive connotations in Lessing's "Jewish self-hatred book." Indeed, Lessing at times suggests "Jewish self-hatred" should have among its references such bleak processes as "self-torturing," and thus he indicates that the phrase's meanings are in some respects not all-too different from those of labels he had long been using. But it is also the case that what Lessing designates as "Jewish self-hatred" isn't simply co-extensive with what he called "self-blaming," "self-contempt," "self-splitting," etc. "Jewish self-hatred" refers, in the end, to something deeper, to a large-scale existential problem that has redemptive promise in Lessing's *Jewish Self-Hatred*. See, for example, the relationship between "*Selbsthaß*" and "*Selbstmäkelei*" (self-skewering) on page 34 of the book. If, like Kuh, Lessing is not always systematic in his usages, "Jewish self-hatred" is *the* term that signifies the big problem that at once generates and will solve itself and help heal the world. Hence the idea that there is in the book *Jewish Self-Hatred* a pattern—whether self-conscious or not—of building on the affirmative meanings that Kuh gave to the term "Jewish self-hatred."

102. See Lessing, *JSH*, 50–51.

103. Theodor Lessing, *Europa und Asien: Untergang der Erde durch Geist* (Leipzig: F. Meiner, 1930), 189.

104. The title of the essay is "Die Unlösbarkeit der Judenfrage," and to be fair, it is not quite as bleak in its outlook as its heading suggests. Lessing, moreover, invokes the same idea in *Jewish Self-Hatred*, the idea, in the first place, being that all national questions are unsolvable as long as people see them as national questions, rather than as a fate-of-all-

humanity issue, since that is really what each national question is, for Lessing. A great recycler, Lessing also reuses in the "Unlösbarkeit" essay some of the key figures from *Jewish Self-Hatred*, including one whereby Jews provide the "serum" that will help the rest of the world overcome its affliction. But this figure is mentioned only in passing in the essay; it is developed more concertedly in the book. The book, furthermore, indicates that healing can happen immediately. The essay suggests that it is way off in the future—there Lessing imagines "happy peoples" coming about only after "thousands of years." See Lessing, *Ich warf eine Flaschenpost ins Eismeer: Essays und Feuilletons (1923–1933)*, ed. Rainer Marwedel (Darmstadt: Luchterhand, 1986), pp. 412–33. To be sure, at least one anti-Zionist reviewer of *Jewish Self-Hatred* found the book unduly pessimistic in its cultural outlook, but here the reviewer projected the tone and the terms of Lessing's earlier work onto the "Jewish self-hatred book," which is something that, as we have seen, readers continue to do. Various continuities invite the move.

105. Lessing, *JSH*, p. 27.

106. Lessing *JSH*, p. 50.

107. Lessing *JSH*, p. 43

108. Jacques Derrida, *Dissemination*, trans. Barbara Johnson, (Chicago: University of Chicago Press, 1979), p. 129.

109. Lessing, *JSH*, p. 217.

110. Quoted in the appendix to Kuh *JD*, p. 180.

111. Anton Kuh, *Luftlinien: Feuilletons, Essays, und Publizistik*, ed. Ruth Greuner (Berlin: Verlag Volk und Welt, 1981), p. 499.

112. Kuh, *Luftlinien*, quoted in Greuner's afterword, p. 507

113. Kuh, *Luftlinien*, p. 505.

114. Neither Gilman nor Volkov nor Finlay mentions Kuh; however, Kuh's coinage and the designs that motivated it haven't gone unnoticed. Andreas Kilcher takes stock of them, for example, in his generally excellent introduction to the reprint edition of *Juden und Deutsche* (1921), the book in which Kuh tries to make the case for "Jewish self-hatred." Ritchie Robertson has noted Kuh's gesture as well in *The 'Jewish Question' in German Literature*, p. 289. And yet neither Kilcher nor Robertson acknowledges the sanguine meanings Kuh tried to inject into his new concept. Indeed, Kilcher (gently) criticizes Gilman for leaving Kuh out of his narrative of the concept "Jewish self-hatred," but he, Kilcher, doesn't suggest that the case of Kuh fundamentally shakes up Gilman's narrative. Kilcher, in fact, sees Weininger's understanding of Jewish self-hatred and Kraus's conception of Jewish antisemitism as

precursors to Kuh's concept, rather than as foils. Several things explain this oversight. Kuh's text is highly, indeed, willfully unsystematic, and his use of "Jewish self-hatred" sometimes resembles what Kraus meant by "Jewish antisemites"—it is a text that lends itself to being quoted out of context. Then there is the fact that Gilman's narrative has become quite entrenched: even Gilman's critics, e.g., Finlay, have relied on it. And even if Gilman's narrative doesn't address Kuh, it creates expectations that foster partial readings of Kuh's text. See Kilcher, "Anton Kuh und sein Essay 'Juden und Deutsche,'" in Kuh *JD*, p. 32, and Robertson, *The 'Jewish Question' in German Literature*, p. 289.

115. Neither Kuh nor Lessing was particularly learned with respect to Judaism and Jewish culture; however, Lessing did have an interest in the culture of Eastern Jewry, and it's possible that in developing his notion of a salutary Jewish self-skewering, he was, in some way, inspired by an awareness of actual traditions of self-critique among the orthodox Jews of Eastern Europe. For example, the Mussar movement, which came about in Lithuania in the nineteenth century, was known for its exalting and ritualizing of ruthless self-criticism. There are, however, basic differences between such valorizing of Jewish self-criticism and Lessing's interpretation of Jewish self-hatred. The former has an ascetic bent; the latter is ultimately presented, as we will see, as a way of getting beyond precisely Jewish asceticism.

116. Freud, "Über den Gegensinn der Urworte," *Gesammelte Werke, chronologisch geordnet*, vol. 8 (Frankfurt: Fischer, 1961), p. 215. I want to thank Stephen Kern for pointing out the affinity between Kuh's use of "Jewish self-hatred" and Freud's *Urworte*.

117. Endelman, "Jewish Self-Hatred in Britain and Germany," p. 333.

118. As I've argued elsewhere, the problem with defensiveness about the term "Jewish self-hatred" in the study of Jewish culture isn't simply that it has resulted in impractical definitions. It has led scholars, more generally, to put their theoretical energy into defining (and redefining) "Jewish self-hatred," when the key challenge in the study of Jewish self-hatred actually lies elsewhere, at least in my estimation. If there is a pressing weakness in this area of inquiry, it isn't that its object has been poorly defined; rather, it's that scholars have been unsystematic in determining antisemitic-seeming utterances by Jews to be (or not to be) expressions of Jewish self-hatred. On this issue, see my essay "The Jewish Self-Hatred Octopus," *The German Quarterly* 82, no. 3 (Summer 2009), pp. 356–73.

119. See Janik, "The Jewish Self-Hatred Hypothesis," p. 80, and Ko-

selleck, *The Practice of Conceptual History*, p. 37. While I agree with Janik's point, his attempt to underpin it is flawed. Janik argues that despite Peter Gay's highly critical attitude toward Lessing, Gay nevertheless took on Lessing's essentialist notion of Jewishness when he adopted Lessing's concept (i.e., "Jewish self-hatred"), for, according to Janik, such meanings can be transmitted in "unconscious" ways. But Janik's evidence for this is dubious. He cites Gay paraphrasing Otto Weininger's understanding of his Jewishness, whereby Jewishness is (alas) "ineradicable," then Janik hastily attributes such thinking about Jewishness to Gay. See Janik, "The Jewish Self-Hatred Hypothesis," p. 80.

120. Volkov, "Selbstgefälligkeit und Selbsthaß," in her *Antisemitismus als kultureller Code* (Munich: Beck, 2000), p. 196.

121. Clement Greenberg, "Self-Hatred and Jewish Chauvinism," *Commentary* 10 (July-December 1950), p. 433. Like Kuh and Lessing, Greenberg isn't always systematic in using "Jewish self-hatred." Indeed, in the first part of his essay, he applies the term both to Jewish chauvinism and "nationalism" and his own, very different outlook, which he sees as more salutary, and which involves antinationalism. By the end of the essay, however, "Jewish self-hatred" is associated primarily with Greenberg's own position.

122. Philip Roth, *Portnoy's Complaint* (New York: Random House, 1969), p. 265.

Part Two: Birth of "Jewish Self-Hatred"

1. *Prager Tagblatt* (December 23, 1919), p. 5.

2. See *Prager Tagblatt* (December 18, 1919), p. 4.

3. Peter Panter (i.e, Kurt Tucholsky), "Auf dem Nachttisch, *Die Weltbühne* 28, no. 5 (February 2, 1932), p. 179.

4. In 1919, Prague witnessed numerous instances of anti-Jewish violence. In November of 1920, there were anti-Jewish riots. See, for example, Christoph Stötzl, *Kafkas böses Böhmen: Zur Sozialgeschichte eines Prager Juden* (Frankfurt: Ullstein, 1989).

5. Much of my reconstruction of this lecture is based on an essay in *Self-Defense*, by Felix Weltsch. Here Weltsch writes that the speaker, i.e., Anton Kuh, "takes as his starting point Jewish antisemitism, which he sees as a perspicacious, self-critical outlook on the part of Jews." In summarizing the review, Kilcher, interestingly, suggests that Weltsch addresses Kuh's "critique of 'Jewish antisemitism' and assimilation," when

Kuh doesn't seem to be offering a critique of Jewish antisemitism. Certainly Weltsch doesn't imply as much. What Kilcher misses, then, is that Kuh appears to be reworking the meaning of "Jewish antisemitism," i.e., trying to inject the term with positive connotations. It appears that he soon decided coining a new term—namely, "Jewish self-hatred"—would be more effective. See Weltsch's review, which is included in Kilcher's edition of *Juden und Deutsche* (pp. 165–68), as well as p. 42 of Kilcher's introduction.

6. *Prager Tagblatt* (January 1, 1920), p. 7.

7. Brod moved in the same Prague cultural Zionist circles as Weltsch and, as it happens, wrote for the *Prager Tagblatt*, as Kuh eventually would (it wasn't where they published their critiques of liberal Jewry, needless to say). Brod also wrote a novel about the scene at the *Tagblatt* in the 1920s, and it offers an evocative, if compact, portrait of Kuh. See Max Brod, *Prager Tagblatt* (Frankfurt: Fischer, 1964).

8. Quoted in Kuh *JD*, p. 160.

9. Minna von Alth's radio program about Kuh, *Die Welt aus Kaffeehaus Perspektive: ein Portrait des Literaten Anton Kuh*, which was broadcast by West German Radio (Cologne) on August 23, 1962, describes Kuh's death as having occurred in this way. A transcript of the program is housed in the library of the Leo Baeck Institute in New York.

10. Franz Werfel, "Anton Kuh," *Aufbau* (January 31, 1941), p. 9.

11. Fred Hildenbrandt, *Ich soll dich grüßen von Berlin 1922–32: Berliner Erinnerungen, ganz und gar unpolitisch* (Munich: Franz Ehrenwirth Verlag, 1984), p. 131.

12. On the Kuh-Kraus feud, see Edward Timms, *Karl Kraus, Apocalyptic Satirist: The Postwar Crisis and the Rise of the Swastika* (New Haven: Yale University Press, 2005), pp. 315–17, though a few of the details in Timms's account are misrepresented there.

13. Kuh, *Luftlinien*, p. 176. The line comes from Kuh's "Der Affe Zarathustras" speech, which is a screed against Kraus.

14. The most extensive biography of Kuh currently available is Ruth Greuner's fine afterword in *Luftlinien*, pp. 499–524. It is the source of much of the biographical information mentioned here. But I have also profited greatly from my correspondence with Walter Schübler, who is writing a life of Kuh, and has been wonderfully generous in sharing his research with me.

15. Kuh, *Luftlinien*, p. 25.

16. Cited in Le Rider, *Modernity and Crisis of Identity*, p. 131.

17. This isn't to intimate that Krafft-Ebing was a great progressive.

However, as Harry Oosterhuis has shown, Krafft-Ebing was somewhat more tolerant of and sympathetic to sexual deviance than he is often made out to have been. See Oosterhuis, *Stepchildren of Nature: Krafft-Ebing, Psychiatry, and the Making of Sexual Identity* (Chicago: University of Chicago Press, 2000).

18. See Le Rider, *Modernity and Crisis of Identity*, pp. 133–35.

19. Cited in Le Rider, *Modernity and Crisis of Identity*, p. 133. Le Rider's section on Gross offers a lucid overview of Gross's career.

20. Otto Gross, "Zur Überwindung der kulturellen Krise," *Die Aktion* 3, no. 14 (April 2, 1913), p. 385

21. Gross, "Zur Überwindung der kulturellen Krise," p. 386.

22. Gross, "Zur Überwindung der kulturellen Krise," p. 387.

23. Gross, "Anmerkungen zu einer neuen Ethik," *Die Aktion* 3, no. 49 (December 6, 1913), p. 1142.

24. Cited in Reiner Stach, *Kafka: Die Jahre der Erkenntnis* (Frankfurt am Main: Fischer, 2008), p. 194.

25. Kuh, *Luftlinien*, pp. 25–26.

26. This isn't to imply that Gross and Marianne Kuh, who was known as Mizzie, were married. As far I as I can tell, they weren't. The daughter they had together was born on November 23, 1916.

27. Cited in Georg Wenzel, ed. *Arnold Zweig 1887–1968: Werk und Leben in Dokumenten und Bildern* (East Berlin: Aufbau, 1978), p. 74.

28. Or more precisely, Kuh's writings were reprinted and sometimes previewed in Zionist newspapers. For example, one of them (the *Jüdische Rundschau*) even ran an excerpt from the anti-Zionist *Jews and Germans*.

29. Max Brod, "Ein Wort über Anton Kuh," reprinted in Kuh *JD*, p. 159.

30. Kuh, Pogrom, *Der Friede* 1, no. 19 (May 31, 1918), pp, 449–50.

31. Cited in Greuner's afterword to *Luftlinien* on p. 507.

32. See Nicholas Fraser, "Man of No Nation," *Harper's Magazine* (January 2009), pp. 76-82.

33. Stefan Zweig, *Die Welt von Gestern: Erinnerungen eines Europäers* (Frankfurt: Suhrkamp, 1996), p. 321.

34. Zweig, *Die Welt von Gestern*, p. 341.

35. Zweig, *Die Welt von Gestern*, p. 345.

36. Kuh, *Luftlinien*, p. 25.

37. This isn't to imply that "Red Vienna" has been outright neglected. There are, in fact, many excellent studies of the topic, including

Timm's *Karl Kraus, Apocalyptic Satirist* and the recent volume edited by Deborah Holmes and Lisa Silverman, *Interwar Vienna: Culture between Tradition and Modernity* (Rochester, N.Y.: Camden House, 2009).

38. Kuh *JD*, p. 108.

39. Kuh *JD*, p. 76. For at least twenty years, a straightforwardly mocking version of the term "Jewish antisemites" had been in circulation—"*antisemitelnde Juden*," which translates as something like "Jews who spew antisemitisms." The coiner of this pejorative phrase appears to be Nathan Birnbaum, the great champion of Yiddish, and, it seems, the coiner also of the term "Zionism."

40. Cited in Greuner's afterword to *Luftlinien* on p. 505. Kuh's term is "*Umwortungen*."

41. Kuh *JD*, p. 121.

42. *JD*, p. 121.

43. *JD*, p. 121.

44. *JD*, p. 92.

45. *JD*, p. 77.

46. *JD*, p. 88.

47. *JD*, p. 89.

48. *JD*, p. 89.

49. *JD*, p. 89.

50. Kilcher helpfully makes the point about *Tikkun* in the introduction to *Jews and Germans* (Kuh *JD*, p. 33). The line about loving each other without violence comes from Kuh's section on Gross—that is, p. 83 of *JD*.

51. Kuh *JD*, p. 76.

52. Kuh *JD*, p. 99.

53. Greenberg, "Self-Hatred and Jewish Chauvinism," p. 433.

54. Kuh *JD*, p. 99.

55. *JD*, p. 77.

56. *JD*, p. 99.

57. *JD*, p. 100.

58. Kraus published his response in *Die Fackel* 561–67 (March 1921), p. 56.

59. Lessing *JD*, p. 79.

60. Karl Kraus, *Literatur order Man wird doch da sehn* in *Dramen*, ed. Christian Wagenknecht (Frankfurt: Suhrkamp, 1987), p. 52.

61. *JD*, pp. 96–97.

62. *JD*, p. 97.

63. *JD*, p. 98.

64. Ritchie Robertson notes this in his *The 'Jewish Question' in German Literature*, p. 287, and I am grateful for the observation.

65. Boelke-Fabian makes this point in "Das Selbst und die Anderen," p. 3. I am grateful for this observation, too.

66. Kuh *JD*, p. 95

67. *JD*, pp. 142–43.

68. *JD*, p. 80.

69. *JD*, p. 81.

70. The line comes from Kilcher's introduction to *Jews and Germans* (Kuh *JD*, p. 21).

71. Kuh *JD*, p. 85. The debate about Jews as the founders of patriarchy didn't end with Kuh, of course. For a critical analysis of a more recent, more feminist version, see Judith Plaskow, "Blaming Jews for Inventing Patriarchy," *Lilith* 7 (1980), especially pp. 11–12.

72. Kuh *JD*, p. 107.

73. *JD*, p. 105.

74. Nietzsche, *Zur Genealogie der Moral*, p. 190.

75. Kuh *JD*, p. 130.

76. *JD*, p. 130.

77. *JD*, pp. 130–31.

78. *JD*, p. 130.

79. Cited in Kuh *JD*, p. 169. Kilcher has done interested readers a great service by including the major reviews of Kuh's *Juden und Deutsche* in an appendix to his edition of Kuh's book.

80. Kuh *JD*, p. 174.

81. *JD*, p. 196.

82. *JD*, p. 189.

83. *JD*, pp. 198–204.

84. *JD*, p. 180.

85. Marwedel, *Theodor Lessing*, p. 355.

Part Three: Prominence

1. Lessing, *Einmal*, p.101.

2. *Einmal*, p. 101.

3. *Einmal*, p. 41.

4. *Einmal*, pp. 50–60.

5. *Einmal*, p. 58.

6. *Einmal*, p. 112.

7. See the chapter "Die Schule" [school], in Lessing, *Einmal*, pp. 104–26.

8. *Einmal*, p. 66.

9. *Einmal*, pp. 99–100.

10. *Einmal*, p. 125.

11. *Einmal*, p. 77–78.

12. Letter to Martin Buber (May 30, 1910). Housed in the Martin Buber papers at the Jerusalem National University Library. MS 3505416. Reading this letter was my first encounter with Lessing's extremely difficult handwriting. Fortunately, Margot Cohen, although mostly retired, happened to be in the manuscripts collection that day, and she very generously helped me to decipher Lessing's script. I want to thank her for that.

13. Lessing, *Intellekt und Selbsthaß*, p. 58.

14. Lessing *JSH*, p. 40.

15. To be more precise, Lessing suggests that certain aspects of his attitude as a youth coincide with what he had written about under the title *Jewish Self-Hatred*. See Lessing, *Einmal*, p. 114.

16. See *Einmal*, pp. 172–87.

17. *Einmal*, p. 172.

18. *Einmal*, p. 203.

19. *Einmal*, p. 203.

20. As far as I can tell, Lessing introduces his argument about the Jews' Aryan heritage, which turns on the claim that Jews intermarried with Persians after the Babylonian captivity, in *Europa und Asien*.

21. *Einmal*, pp. 382–83.

22. *Einmal*, pp. 415–28.

23. Cited in Frederic V. Grunfeld, *Prophets without Honor: A Background to Freud, Kafka, Einstein and Their World* (New York: Holt, Rinehart, Winston, 1979), p. 82.

24. Hans Mayer, *Außenseiter* (Frankfurt am Main: Suhrkamp, 1975), pp. 414–21.

25. Lawrence Baron, "Theodor Lessing: Between Jewish Self-Hatred and Zionism," pp. 323–40.

26. Baron, "Theodor Lessing," p. 323.

27. Baron, "Theodor Lessing," p. 337.

28. Baron, "Theodor Lessing," p. 338.

29. Baron, "Theodor Lessing," p. 340.

30. Like Gilman's book, Baron's article stresses precisely the conti-

nuity between Lessing's late study *Jewish Self-Hatred* and his fin-de-siècle works. Baron writes about an essay of 1901 that it "is his [Lessing's] first analysis of Jewish self-hatred and anticipates his later study of that problem." See Baron, "Theodor Lessing," p. 336 (note 85).

31. Gay, *Freud, Jews and Other Germans*, p. 195.

32. See Groys's forward to the 1984 edition of Lessing, *Der jüdische Selbsthaß*, p. xxv.

33. Lessing, letter of April 8, 1928, to "Fräulein" Breling of the Central Association of German Citizens of the Jewish Faith, in Stadtarchiv Hannover, Theodor Lessing *Nachlaß* 888.

34. Lessing, *Europa und Asien*, p. 127.

35. Lessing, letter to Brod of March 6, 1923; housed in the Theodor Lessing Collection at the Leo Baeck Institute in New York, AR 980 autographs folder. Lessing is referring here to the third edition of *Europe and Asia*. The title was later changed again; *Europe and Asia* became the main title once more, and *The Decline of the Earth through Mind* was relegated to subtitle status. The reason for the second shift isn't readily apparent; however, it could have had something to do with the similarity between the title *The Decline of the Earth through Mind* and Klages's title *The Mind as the Enemy of the Soul*. Certainly the timing is suggestive: Lessing went back to *Europa and Asia* just around the time Klages's work appeared.

36. Lessing *JSH*, p. 40.

37. Rainer Marwedel, *Theodor Lessing*, p. 55.

38. Lessing, *Europa und Asien*, p. 6.

39. Lessing, *Einmal*, p. 250.

40. *Einmal*, p. 250.

41. *Einmal*, p. 252.

42. *Einmal*, p. 397.

43. Lessing, "Ludwig Jakobowski," *Ost und West* 1, no. 8 (August 1901), p. 562.

44. Lessing, "Ludwig Jakobowski," pp. 562–65.

45. Lessing, "Ludwig Jakobowski," pp. 571–75.

46. Lessing, "Ludwig Jakobowski," p. 568.

47. Moritz Goldstein, "Deutsch-jüdische Parnaß" [The German-Jewish Parnassus], *Der Kunstwart: Halbmonatsschau für Ausdruckskultur auf allen Lebensgebieten* 25, no.11 (March 1912), pp. 281–312.

48. Lessing, "Jiddisches Theater in London," *Die Shaubühne* 6, no. 17 (April 28, 1910), p. 455.

49. Cited in Marwedel, *Theodor Lessing*, p. 76.

50. Lessing, "Eindrücke aus Galizien," reprinted in Jochen Hartwig, *"Sei was immer du bist:" Theodor Lessings wendungsvolle Identitätsbildung als Deutscher und Jude* (Oldenberg: Bis, 1999), pp. 208–9.

51. Lessing, "Eindrücke," p. 218.

52. Lessing, "Eindrücke," p. 221.

53. Lessing, "Eindrücke," p. 221.

54. To be sure, Lessing does remark that the *Ostjuden* of Galicia are "at bottom a people made up of run-down aristocrats." But the suggestion that Jews had become physically and spiritually run-down was a kind of mantra of turn-of-the-century cultural Zionism, and the position Lessing takes here clearly doesn't involve or amount to an arresting, overdetermined projection of Teutonic virtues onto the Jews of the past. See "Eindrücke," p. 224.

55. Lessing, "Samuel zieht die Bilanz," reprinted in Hartwig, *"Sei was immer du bist,"* p. 239.

56. Kraus's rhyme, in "Heine and the Consequences," reads, "Itzig Witzig." "Itzak Wisecrack" is Jonathan Franzen's brilliant rendering; Franzen's English translation of "Heine and the Consequences" is forthcoming. For an analysis of the polemical language in "Heine and the Consequences," see my book *The Anti-Journalist: Karl Kraus and Jewish Self-Fashioning in Fin-de-siècle Europe* (Chicago: University of Chicago Press, 2008), pp. 96–106.

57. See Reitter, *The Anti-Journalist*, pp. 90–91.

58. Alfred Kerr, "Glossen," *Pan* (July 1, 1911), p. 581.

59. For more information about Kraus's feuds with Harden and Kerr, as well as about the reception of "Heine and the Consequences," see Reitter, *The Anti-Journalist*, pp. 88–96.

60. See Hermann Kurzke, *Thomas Mann: Life as a Work of Art*, trans. Leslie Wilson (Princeton: Princeton University Press, 2002), pp. 206–10; and Jacques Darmaun, "Thomas Manns Polemik mit Theodor Lessing," in *"Sinngebung des Sinnlosen:" Zum Leben und Werk des Kritikers Theodor Lessing*, ed. Elke-Vera Kotowski (Hildesheim, Zurich, New York: Olms, 2006), pp. 165–80. The quotations come from Kurzke's text.

61. Kurzke, *Thomas Mann*, p. 208.

62. Cited in Kurzke, *Thomas Mann*, p. 209.

63. Lessing, "Samuel," p. 238.

64. Lessing, "Samuel," p. 236.

65. Lessing, "Samuel," p. 237.

66. Lessing, "Samuel Lublinski," reprinted in *"Sei was immer du bist,"* p. 249.

67. Marwedel, *Theodor Lessing*, p. 119.

68. Lessing, "Jude und Kunstleistung," reprinted in *"Sei was immer du bist,"* pp. 265–68.

69. Lessing, *Intellekt und Selbsthaß*, p. 13.

70. Lessing, *Intellekt und Selbsthaß*, p. 19.

71. Lessing, *Intellekt und Selbsthaß*, p. 32.

72. Lessing, *Intellekt und Selbsthaß*, p. 47.

73. Reprinted in *"Sei was immer du bist,"* pp. 283–87. See pp. 284–85.

74. *"Sei was immer du bist,"* p. 285.

75. Lessing, Jüdisches Schicksal," reprinted in *"Sei was immer du bist,"* p. 272.

76. Lessing, "Jüdisches Schicksal," p. 274.

77. Lessing, "Jüdisches Schicksal," pp. 274–75.

78. Cited in Marwedel, *Theodor Lessing*, p. 146.

79. Lessing, "Jüdisches Schicksal," p. 271.

80. Lessing, *Europa und Asien*, p. 217.

81. In his autobiography, it is worth noting, Lessing writes of his early intuition whereby his "powerful will to *Geist*" and his desire for "life immediacy" would be able to interact productively, if perhaps also explosively, like a combustible combination of gases coming into contact with each other. The implication is that unlike Klages, Lessing hoped for, and thought he could work to make fecund, the relationship between *Geist* and life. See Lessing, *Einmal*, p. 250.

82. Lessing, *Einmal*, p. 14.

83. Lessing *JSH*, pp. 9–17.

84. *JSH*, p. 40.

85. *JSH*, p. 17.

86. *JSH*, p. 23.

87. *JSH*, p. 28. Lessing, who was keenly interested in animal psychology, is intimating that with animals, too, submitting to the demands of culture can make for a surfeit of self-awareness and the following concomitant of that: minds turned unhealthily against life.

88. *JSH*, p. 36.

89. *JSH*, p. 43.

90. Lessing further sets up this shift by stating early on that "self-hatred" entails *Geist* becoming a "tyrant over the preconscious life that

carries it," and "yet also" the "desiring and willfully value-creating person getting the upper hand over the logical and logically judging one." For here Lessing appears to be suggesting that the victory of *Geist* is no simple one—and not simply a loss for "life." See Lessing *JSH*, p. 34.

91. Lessing *JSH*, p. 214.

92. *JSH*, p. 43.

93. *JSH*, p. 215.

94. *JSH*, p. 217.

95. *JSH*, p. 217. When I speak of Lessings's "letting go," I mean that he does this relative to what he does elsewhere, and in *Jewish Self-Hatred*, he waffles a little on the question of *Geist* even after the passage in which he frames the Jews' *Geistigkeit* as the solution to the problem that produces it. That is, he goes on to speak, as he had before, of the hollowness of the Jews' cultural accomplishments. But these remarks are brief. After making them, Lessing asserts that he just pointed out how the "sickness of self-hatred" can be "healed." And Lessing ends on an upbeat. In very last passage of the book, Lessing, having accepted the inevitability of *Geist*, proceeds to sound the line that the "nationality question" can be solved through a "strong resolution." See Lessing *JSH*, pp. 222–23. To add a final observation to this note, in the passage about the Jews functioning as a vaccine, Lessing was likely playing off of a recent cultural memory. In 1918, an outbreak of influenza killed more than twenty million people across Europe; it turned out that the best cure was a blood transfusion—a blood transfusion in which the blood came from someone who had had the illness and survived.

Conclusion

1. See, for example, Frederick Cooper with Rogers Brubaker, "Identity," in Cooper, *Colonialism in Question: Theory, Knowledge, Concepts* (Berkeley: University of California Press, 2005), pp. 59–90; and Scott Spector, "Forget Assimilation: Introducing Subjectivity to Jewish History," *Jewish History* 20, nos. 3–4 (2006), pp. 349–61.

2. Cooper and Brubaker, as well as Spector, discuss whether the terms they consider line up with, or effectively evoke, the ideas we have come to attach to them. They also consider alternative possibilities, and thereby work toward improvement. Critics of "Jewish self-hatred" often do neither of these things.

3. See h-net.msu.edu/cgi-bin/logbrowse.pl?trx=vx&list=h-sae&mo
nth=9605&week=e&msg=HvMZnzAc2V4sGOz6kAUopw&user=
&pw=.

4. To be sure, Janik claims, toward the conclusion of his essay, that he doesn't want his argument to be simply "nihilistic." And to this end, he offers some thoughts about what the "concept self-hatred" has meant in different kinds of discussions and in different academic disciplines, the idea being that it would be helpful to keep its different uses and meanings straight. But soon thereafter we find him reasserting his point about how we would likely be better off if we stopped using "Jewish self-hatred" as an analytic category in intellectual history: "In the history of ideas self-hatred obscures as much—or more—than it illuminates." Janik, "The Jewish Self-Hatred Hypothesis," p. 86–87.

5. To acknowledge this point, as I readily did in chapter 1, isn't necessarily to endorse the reasoning behind it. Janik, as we know, has made much of the double life of "Jewish self-hatred" as a scholarly concept and popular term, or as a "category of analysis" and "category of practice." What he has maintained is that generally speaking, scholars haven't been in control of the exchange between those two levels of use, so potent and firmly embedded are the term's polemical Ur-meanings. Where they are explicitly critical of these meanings, according to Janik, they have managed to take them on, for linguistic transmission can happen unconsciously (hence the idea of scholars not being in control of the semantic exchange that they are themselves effecting). This is an intriguing claim, as I noted in part 1. No doubt the histories of words sometimes do pull users in this or that direction. However, Janik has gone so far as to make a deterministic argument, whereby users seem unable to resist the pull of a history even when they reflect on that history self-consciously. And, again, Janik's attempt to make this argument stick is less than convincing. See Janik, "The Jewish Self-Hatred Hypothesis," p. 80.

6. Gilman, *Jewish Self-Hatred*, p. 2.

7. Gilman, *Jewish Self-Hatred*, p. 1.

8. Gilman also speaks of Jewish self-hatred as having to do with an "illusionary definition of the self." See Gilman, *Jewish Self-Hatred*, p. 2. Accordingly, he leaves mostly open the question of how the Jewish self-hatred of the luminaries he discusses may have fostered their successes.

9. Volkov, Excurus," p. 37.

10. Volkov, "Excursus," p. 40.

11. Volkov, "Excursus," p. 44. Volkov's "Excursus" essay is a reworking of an earlier essay, which I cited in part 1 of this book, and in which Volkov's use of "Jewish self-hatred" isn't quite so restrictive.

12. Kraus, *Die Fackel* 339–40 (December 30, 1911), p. 2.

13. On this aspect of Kraus's work, as well as Kafka's, Benjamin's and Scholem's responses to Kraus, see chapters 2 through 4 of my book *The Anti-Journalist*.

14. For a recent philosophical take on the characteristics of hatred, which, unfortunately, hasn't been translated into English, see Aurel Kolnai, *Hochmut, Ekel, Haß: Zur Phänomenologie feindlicher Gefühle* (Frankfurt am Main: Suhrkamp, 2007).

15. Walter Benjamin, "Karl Kraus," *Illuminationen*, ed. Siegfried Unseld (Frankfurt: Suhrkamp, 1977), p. 348.

16. Kraus, "Er ist doch e Jud," in *Untergang der Welt durch Schwarze Magie*, ed. Christian Wagenknecht (Frankfurt am Main: Suhrkamp, 1989), p. 330.

17. Kraus, *Aphorismen*, ed. Wagenknecht (Frankfurt am Main: Suhrkamp, 1986), p. 270.

Arendt, Hannah. *The Jew as Pariah: Jewish Identity and Politics in the Modern Age*. Edited by Ronald Feldman. New York: Grove Press, 1978.

———. *Rahel Varnhagen: The Life of a Jewess*. Edited by Liliane Weissberg; translated by Richard and Clara Winston. Baltimore: Johns Hopkins University Press, 1997.

Aschheim, Steven. *Brothers and Strangers: The Eastern Jew in German and German Jewish Consciousness, 1800–1923*. Madison: University of Wisconsin Press, 1982.

Berlin, Isaiah. "Benjamin Disraeli, Karl Marx, and the Search for Identity." Pp. 252–86 in Berlin, *Against the Current: Essays in the History of Ideas*. Edited by Henry Hardy. New York: Penguin Books, 1980.

Bernstein, Michael André. *Foregone Conclusion: Against Apocalyptic History*. Berkeley: University of California Press, 1994.

Baron, Lawrence. "Theodor Lessing: Between Assimilation and Zionism." *Leo Baeck Institute Yearbook* 26 (1981): 323–40.

Boelke-Fabian, Andrea. "Das Selbst und die Anderen: Über das Dilemma der Ambilanz und die schwierige philosophische Selbstbestimmung von Deutschsein und Judesein zwischen Mythos und Projektion. Theodor Lessings Essay *Der jüdische Selbsthaß* und seine Autobiographie *Einmal und nie wieder*." Ph.D. diss., Johann Wolfgang Goethe-Universität, Frankfurt am Main, 2003.

Conard, R. C. Review of *The Anti-Journalist*, published, in 2008, in *Choice Reviews* online at www.cro2.org/default.aspx?page=review display&pid=3392352.

Cooper, Frederick, with Rogers Brubaker. "Identity." Pp. 59–90 in Cooper, *Colonialism in Question: Theory, Knowledge, History*. University of California Press: Berkeley, 2005.

———. "Modernity." Pp. 113–52 in Cooper, *Colonialism in Question:*

Theory, Knowledge, History. University of California Press: Berkeley, 2005.

Darmaun, Jacques. "Thomas Manns Polemik mit Theodor Lessing." Pp. 165–80 in *"Sinngebung des Sinnlosen:" Zum Leben und Werk des Kritikers Theodor Lessing*. Edited by Elke-Vera Kotowski. Hildesheim, Zurich, and New York: Olms, 2006.

Du Bois, W.E.B. *The Souls of Black Folk*. New York: Vintage, 1990.

Endelman, Todd. "Jewish Self-Hatred in Britain and Germany." Pp. 331–65 in *Two Nations: British and German Jews in Comparative Perspective*, edited by Michael Brenner et al. Tübingen: Mohr, 1999.

Finlay, W.M.F. "Pathologizing Dissent: Zionism, Identity Politics, and the 'Self-Hating Jew.'" *British Journal of Social Psychology* 44 (2005): 201–22.

Freud, Sigmund. *Freud, Der Mann Moses und die Monotheistische Religion*. Pp. 103–246 in *Sigmund Freuds Gesammelte Werke, Chronologisch geordnet*, vol. 16. Frankfurt am Main: Suhrkamp, 1966.

Gay, Peter. "Hermann Levi: A Study in Service and Self-Hatred." Pp. 189–230 in Gay, *Freud, Jews and Other Germans: Masters and Victims in Modernist Culture*. Oxford and New York: Oxford University Press, 1978.

Gilman, Sander. *Jewish Self-Hatred: Anti-Semitism and the Hidden Language of the Jews*. Baltimore: Johns Hopkins University Press, 1986.

Glenn, Susan. "The Vogue of Jewish Self-Hatred in Post–World War Two America." *Jewish Social Studies* 12, no. 3 (Spring/Summer 2006), pp. 95–136.

Golomb, Jacob. "Jewish Self-Hatred: Nietzsche, Freud, and the Case of Theodor Lessing." *Leo Baeck Institute Yearbook* 50 (2005): 233–45.

Greenberg. Clement. "Self-Hatred and Jewish Chauvinism." *Commentary 10* (July–December 1950), pp. 426–33.

Grunfeld, Frederic. *Prophets without Honor: A Background to Freud, Kafka, Einstein, and Their World*. New York: Holt, Rinehart, Winston, 1979.

Hartwig, Jochen. *"Sei was immer du bist:" Theodor Lessings wendungsvolle Identitätsbildung als Deutscher und Jude*. Oldenberg: Bis, 1999. This volume includes reprinted versions of most of Lessing's essays about Jewish topics, such as his portraits of Samuel Lublinski and the Jews of Galicia, and his articles on Zionism.

Hellige, Hans D. "Generationskonflkt, Selbsthaß, und die Entstehung antikapitalistischer Positionen im Judentum." *Geschichte und Gesellschaft* 5, no. 4 (1979): 476–518

Herzl, Theodor. *AltNeuland*. Norderstedt: haGalil, 2004.

Hess, Jonathan. *Middlebrow Literature and the Making of German-Jewish Identity*. Stanford: Stanford University Press, 2010.

Hildenbrandt, Fred. "Geschichten von Anton Kuh." Pp. 128–33 in Hildenbrandt, *Ich soll dich grüßen von Berlin, 1922–1932: Berliner Erinnerungen ganz und gar unpolitisch*. Munich: Franz Ehrenwirth Verlag, 1966.

Janik, Allan. "Viennese Culture and the Jewish Self-Hatred Hypothesis: A Critique." Pp. 75–88 in *Jews, Anti-Semitism, and Culture in Vienna*, edited by Ivar Oxaar et al. New York and London: Routledge, 1987.

Kilcher, Andreas. "Anti-Ödipus im Lande der Ur-Väter: Franz Kafka und Anton Kuh." Pp. 41–65 in *"Ich bin Ende und Anfang": Franz Kafka, Zionism and Beyond.*, edited by Mark Gelber. Tübingen: Niemeyer, 2003.

Klages, Ludwig. *Der Geist als Widersacher der Seele*. Bonn: Grundmann, 1981.

Koselleck, Reinhart. *The Practice of Conceptual History: Timing History, Spacing Concepts*. Translated by Todd Presner and Kirsten Behnke. Stanford: Stanford University Press, 2002.

Kraus, Karl. Untitled essay. *Die Fackel* 11 (Mid-July 1899), pp. 1–4.

———. *Eine Krone für Zion*. In Kraus, *Frühe Schriften*, vol. 2. Edited by J. J. Braakenburg. Munich: Kösel, 1979.

———. *Aphorismen*, ed. Christian Wagenknecht. Frankfurt am Main: Suhrkamp, 1986.

———. *Literatur oder Man wird doch da sehn*. In Kraus, *Dramen*. Edited by Christian Wagenknecht. Frankfurt am Main: Suhrkamp, 1987.

———. "Heine und die Folgen." Pp. 185–210 in Kraus, *Untergang der Welt durch Schwarze Magie*, edited by Christian Wagenknecht. Frankfurt am Main: Suhrkamp, 1989.

Kuh, Anton. *Luftlinien: Feuilletons, Essays und Publizistik*. Edited by Ruth Greuner. Berlin: Verlag Volk und Welt, 1981.

———. *Zeitgeist im Literaturcafe: Feuilletons, Essays und Publizistik*. Edited by Ulrike Lehner. Vienna: Löcker Verlag, 1983.

———. *Juden und Deutsche*. Edited by Andreas Kilcher. Vienna: Löcker, 2003.

Kurzke, Hermann. *Thomas Mann: Life as a Work of Art*. Translated by Leslie Wilson. Princeton: Princeton University Press, 2002.

Langmuir, Gavin. *Toward a Definition of Antisemitism*. Berkeley: University of California Press, 1990.

Lensing, Leo. "Fackel-Leser und Werfel-Verehrer: Anmerkungen zu Kafkas Briefen an Robert Klopstock." In *Kafkas letzter Freund*, edited by Hugo Wetscherek, Vienna: Inlibris, 2003.

Le Rider, Jacques. *Modernity and Crises of Identity.* Translated by Rosemary Morris. New York: Continuum, 1991.

Lessing, Theodor. *Der Lärm: Eine Kampschrift gegen die Geräusche unseres Lebens.* Wiesbaden: J. F. Bergmann, 1908.

———. *Philosophie als Tat.* Göttingen: Härnke, 1914.

———. *Geschichte als Sinngebung des Sinnlosen: oder die Geburt der Geschichte aus dem Mythos.* Leipzig: Reinicke, 1927.

———. *Der jüdische Selbsthaß.* Berlin: Jüdischer Verlag, 1930.

———. *Europa und Asien: Der Untergang der Erde durch Geist.* Leipzig: F. Meiner, 1930.

———. *Einmal und nie wieder.* Gütersloh: Bertelsmann, 1969.

———. *Die verfluchte Kultur: Gedanken über den Gegensatz von Leben und Geist.* Munich: Matthes & Seitz, 1981.

———. *Der jüdische Selbsthaß. Mit einem Essay von Boris Groys.* Munich: Matthes & Seitz, 1984.

———. *Nietzsche.* Munich: Matthes & Seitz, 1985.

———. *'Ich warf eine Flaschenpost ins Eismeer': Essays und Feuilletons (1923–1933).* Edited by Rainer Marwedel. Darmstadt: Luchterhand, 1986.

Lewin, Kurt. "Self-Hatred among Jews." Pp. 186–200 in Lewin, *Resolving Social Conflicts & Field and Theory in Social Science.* Washington, D.C.: American Psychological Association, 1997.

Loewenberg, Peter, "Antisemitismus und jüdischer Selbsthaß: Eine sich wechselseitig verstärkende sozialpsychologische Doppelbeziehung." *Geschichte und Gesellschaft* 5, no. 4 (1979), pp. 455–75.

Mamet, David. *The Wicked Son: Anti-Semitism, Self-Hatred, and the Jews.* New York: Schocken, 2006.

Marwedel, Rainer. *Theodor Lessing, 1872–1933: Eine Biographie.* Darmstadt and Neuwied: Luchterhand, 1987.

Mayer, Hans. "Theodor Lessing: Ein Bericht über ein politisches Trauma." Pp. 94–120 in Mayer, *Der Repräsentant und der Märtyrer: Konstellationen der Literatur.* Frankfurt am Main: Suhrkamp, 1971.

———. *Außenseiter.* Frankfurt am Main: Suhrkamp, 1975.

Mendes-Flohr, Paul. *Divided Passions: Jewish Intellectuals and the Experience of Modernity.* Detroit: Wayne State University Press, 1991.

Philippson, Ludwig. *Förderung und Hemmniß: Eine Skizze aus dem Leben.*

Pp. 217–61 in Philippson, *Saron: Novellenbuch*, vol. 2. Lepizig: Leopold Schauß Verlag, 1856.

Radkau, Joachim. *Das Zeitalter der Nervosität: Deutschland zwischen Bismarck und Hitler*. Munich: Hanser, 1998.

Reitter, Paul. *The Anti-Journalist: Karl Kraus and Jewish Self-Fashioning in Fin-de-Siècle Europe*. Chicago: University of Chicago Press, 2008.

Robertson, Ritchie. *The "Jewish Question" in German Literature: Emancipation and Its Discontents, 1749–1939*. Cambridge and New York: Cambridge University Press, 1999.

Rose, Jacqueline. "The Myth of Jewish Self-Hatred." *The Guardian* (February 2007) online at www.guardian.co.uk/commentisfree/2007/feb/08/holdjewishvoices6.

Roth, Philip. *Portnoy's Complaint*. New York, Random House, 1969.

Schnitzler, Arthur. *Der Weg ins Freie*. In *Gesammelte Werke von Arthur Schnitzler in zwei Abteilung*, part 1, vol. 3. Berlin: Fischer, 1912.

Schreiber, Emanuel. *Die Selbstkritik der Juden*. Berlin: Duncker's Verlag, 1880.

Spector, Scott. "Forget Assimilation: Introducing Subjectivity to Jewish History." *Jewish History* 20, nos. 3–4 (2006), pp. 349–61.

Stach, Reiner. *Kafka: Die Jahre der Erkenntnis*. Frankfurt am Main: Fischer, 2008.

Timms, Edward. *Karl Kraus: Apocalyptic Satirist. Vol. 2. The Postwar Crisis and the Rise of the Swastika*. New Haven: Yale University Press, 2005.

———. "Cultural Parameters between the Wars: A Reassessment of the Vienna Circles." Pp. 21–31 in *Interwar Vienna: Culture between Tradition and Modernity*, edited by Deborah Holmes and Lisa Silverman. Rochester, N.Y.: Camden House, 2009.

Volkov, Shulamit. *Antisemitismus als kultureller Code: Zehn Essays*. Munich: Beck, 2000.

———. "Excursus on Self-Hatred and Self-Criticism." Pp. 33–46 in Volkov, *Germans, Jews, and Antisemites: Trials in Emancipation*. Cambridge: Cambridge University Press: 2006.

Weininger, Otto. *Sex and Character: An Investigation of Fundamental Principles*. Translated by Ladislaus Löb. Bloomington: Indiana University Press, 2005.

Wistrich, Robert. "Zionism and Its Jewish Critics (1897–1948)." *Jewish Social Studies* 44, no. 2 (Winter 1998), pp. 68–96.

Adler, Alfred, 59
Advancement and Hindrance
    (Philippson), 19–21
Ahrweiler, Antonie, 77–79
Anton Reiser (Moritz), 68
Auerbach, Berthold, 15
Axelrod, David, 13

Bahr, Hermann, 24, 60
Baptized Jew, The (Wittels), 31–32
Baron, Lawrence, 86–88, 124
Bartels, Adolf, 97
Becher, Johannes R., 56
Bendavid, Lazarus, 17, 18, 133–34n46
Benjamin, Walter, 11, 99, 126, 131n23
Bettauer, Hugo, 60
Blei, Franz, 56
"Blood of the Walsungs, The"
    (Mann), 25–27
Boelke-Fabian, Andrea, 138n98,
    139n100, 146n65
Börne, Ludwig, 15, 40, 122
Brod, Max, 6, 38, 48, 57, 72, 73, 90,
    128–29n3, 130n5, 143n7
Buber, Martin, 7, 32, 33, 57, 72, 81
Buddenbrooks (Mann), 68, 104, 107

Chamberlain, Houston Stewart, 108,
    125
Conard, R. C., 14
Crown for Zion, A (Kraus), 23

"Degeneration and Deportation"
    (Hans Gross), 54
Döblin, Alfred, 3

Emanuel, Rahm, 13
Endelman, Todd, 14, 41–42; use of
    "Jewish self-hatred," 14, 41–42

Finlay, W.M.F., 14–16, 41, 122, 140–
    41n114
Fliess, Wilhelm, 31, 136–37n75
Fraser, Nicholas, 58–59
Freud, Sigmund, 7, 9, 28–31, 40, 41;
    on antisemitism, 28–30
Fritsch, Theodor, 99

Gay, Peter, 9–10, 30, 87, 142n119; use
    of "Jewish self-hatred," 9–10
Gilman, Sander, 14–15, 34, 35, 122–
    23, 125, 126, 132n32, 137n93,
    140–41n114, 147n30, 152n8; on
    the genealogy of "Jewish self-
    hatred," 34, 35; use of "Jewish
    antisemitism," 122; use of "Jewish
    self-hatred," 14–15, 122–23
Goethe, J. W., 68, 71, 82, 95, 97, 103,
    112
Goldmann, Felix, 8–9, 12
Greenberg, Clement, 44, 66, 142n21;
    use of "Jewish self-hatred," 44, 66,
    142n21
Gross, Hans, 54–56
Gross, Otto, 4, 52–57, 60–61, 63, 64,
    66, 68, 72
Groys, Boris, 87

Harden, Maximilian, 54, 104
Hausmann, Raoul, 45
Hebbel, Friedrich, 95, 97

Hegel, G.W.F., 18

Heine, Heinrich, 10, 15, 18, 27, 76, 97, 104, 122, 123, 126

Herzl, Theodor, 23–24, 132n41; use of "Jewish antisemitism," 23

Hess, Jonathan, 19, 135n50

Heyse, Paul, 97

Hirsch, Samson Raphael, 22

Hoddis, Jakob von, 56

Jacobowski, Ludwig, 94–97, 103, 109

Janik, Allan, 9–12, 13, 14, 15, 41, 42, 122, 131n22, 142n119, 152n4, 152n5

"Jewish antisemitism": birth of, 22–23; objections to, 23, 62; popularization of, 23–24

"Jewish self-hatred": the birth of, 2–3, 35, 38–40, 61–71; genealogies of, 10–12, 14–16, 33–35, 36, 121–22; objections to, 2, 9–11, 12, 13–15, 41–42, 67, 121; the pre-history of, 16–35

Jews' State, The (Herzl), 23

Jordan, Wilhelm, 83

Journal of the Fight against the Will for Power, 60–61

Judt, Tony, 13

Jung, Carl, 53

Jung, Franz, 55

Kafka, Franz, 6, 15, 49, 56, 61, 67, 124, 126

Kaznelson, Siegmund, 5–6

Kerr, Alfred, 50, 104

Kilcher, Andreas, 69, 140–41n114, 142–143n5, 145n50

Klages, Ludwig, 32, 82–87, 89, 114, 148n35, 150n89

Kleist, Heinrich von, 96, 97

Kornfeld, Paul, 56

Koselleck, Reinhart, 16, 43

Kraft-Ebbing, Richard von, 54

Kraus, Karl, 10, 14, 15, 23, 35, 45, 51, 66–67, 69, 71, 88, 103–4, 116–17, 125–26, 128–29n3, 131n23, 132n41, 140–41n114, 143n12, 149n56, 149n59, 153n13; use of

"Jewish antisemitism," 23; use of "Jewish self-hatred," 67

Kuh, Anton: on antisemitism 47, 57, 63–65, 68; on "Jewish antisemitism," 62; use of "Jewish self-hatred," 3, 4, 39–40, 61–71, 125— works by: "How I Will Survive Hitler," 49; *Jews and Germans*, 3, 4, 39–40, 61–71, 72, 73, 90, 125, 128n3; "On Sexual Revolution," 46; "Pogrom," 58, 61; "The Summer Lush," 52; "The Tragedy of the Jews," 47–49, 72; "Wedekind," 52; "Zarathustra's Ape," 50, 51

Kuh, David, 51–52

Kuh, Emil, 52

Lasker-Schüler, Else, 56

Le Rider, Jacques, 10, 144n19

Lehmann, Marcus, 22

Lessing, Adele, 76, 78–79, 80, 95

Lessing, Sigmund, 76–80

Lessing, Theodor: on antisemitism, 98, 108, 115–16; use of "Jewish self-hatred," 3, 4, 8, 11–12, 35–38, 114–19—works by: *Europe and Asia*, 89, 90, 92, 113–14, 148n35; "The Fate of the Jews," 112–13; "Impressions from Galicia," 101–3; *Jewish Self-Hatred*, 4, 5–8, 11–12, 34, 35–38, 41, 73, 81, 87–88, 89–91, 114–19; "Ludwig Jakobowski," 94–97, 103, 109; *Once and Never Again*, 75, 81, 82, 83, 92, 93; *Philosophy as Deed*, 75, 92, 108–10, 124; "Samuel Takes Stock," 103, 106–7

Levi, Hermann, 9–10

Lewin, Kurt, 15, 18–19, 28, 122, 134n48; use of "Jewish self-hatred," 18–19, 28, 122

Lietz, Hermann, 99

Limbaugh, Rush, 13

Literature (Kraus), 67

Loos, Adolf, 60

Lublinski, Samuel, 33, 81, 103–7, 137n86

Mamet, David, 13
Mann, Thomas, 25–27, 33, 45, 68, 104–6, 107
Marr, Wilhelm, 22
Marwedel, Rainer, 92, 108, 137n86
Marx, Karl, 15, 122, 134n48
Mayer, Hans, 86, 131n22
Mendelssohn, Moses, 15, 47
Mendes-Flohr, Paul, 14
"'Modern'" (Wagner), 25
Moritz, Karl Philipp, 68
Moses and Monotheism (Freud), 29–30, 41
Musil, Robert, 58–59, 60, 127n2

Netanyahu, Benjamin, 13
Nietzsche, Friedrich, 4, 5, 23, 32, 39, 53, 54, 56, 60, 61, 70–71, 82, 100, 113, 116, 125, 127n2, 133n46, 135n59
Novalis, 68

Old-New Land (Herzl), 24
On the Genealogy of Morals (Nietzsche), 70
"On Overcoming the Crisis of Culture" (Otto Gross), 55
"Our Prospects" (Treitschke), 25

"Paternal Violence" (Otto Gross), 54
Pfemfert, Franz, 53
Philippson, Ludwig, 19, 21
Portnoy's Complaint (Roth), 44
"Prejudgments" (Philippson), 21
Psychopathological Inferiorities (Otto Gross), 54

Rathenau, Walther, 42
"Remarks on a New Ethics," (Otto Gross), 55
Robertson, Ritchie, 140n114, 146n64
Rose, Jacqueline, 13
Roth, Joseph, 39
Roth, Philip, 12, 44

Schenker, Anatol, 129n2
Schnitzler, Arthur, 27–28
Scholem, Gershom, 7, 75, 124, 126

Schreiber, Emanuel, 24–25
Schübler, Walter, 143n14
Self-Criticism of the Jews, The (Schreiber), 24–25
Sex and Character (Weininger), 10, 30–31
Simmel, Georg, 33, 81, 109
Simon, Ezechial, 76
Soros, George, 13
Spir, Afrikan, 92
Steiner, Rudolf, 96
Sternheim, Carl, 76
Sternheim, Julius Carl, 76
Swoboda, Hermann, 30, 136–37n75

To Reap and to Sow (Lehmann), 22
Treitschke, Heinrich von, 104–5, 108

Varnhagen, Rahel, 18–19, 42
Victory of Jewry over the Germans, The (Marr), 22
Vienna (Bahr), 24
Viertel, Berthold, 50, 129n3
Volkov, Shulamit, 14, 35–36, 43, 123–24, 125, 140n114, 153n11; on the genealogy of "Jewish self-hatred," 34–35; use of "Jewish self-hatred," 14, 43, 123–24

Wagner, Richard, 10, 25, 27, 31, 100
Wassermann, Jakob, 42, 103, 124
Webern, Anton, 60
Weininger, Otto, 10, 11–12, 28, 30–31, 68, 116, 123, 136n75, 137, 140–41n114, 142n119; on anti-semitism, 31
Weltsch, Felix, 6, 48–49, 62, 72, 142–43n5, 143n7
Weltsch, Robert, 6, 72, 73
Werfel, Franz, 49, 50, 54, 57, 60–61, 63, 64, 67
Wittels, Fritz, 31–32
Wittgenstein, Ludwig, 59, 103
Wolfskehl, Karl, 76
Wolfskehl, Otto Wilhelm, 76

Zweig, Arnold, 29, 57, 128–29n3
Zweig, Stefan, 59

ACKNOWLEDGMENTS

Like a lot of books, *On the Origins of Jewish Self-Hatred* began as a conversation. In this case, however, the initial conversation ran until the final word had been written, because my initial conversation partner became my editor—and what an editor she was. Brigitta van Rheinberg did much more than help put the project into motion and offer useful advice as, by turns, the manuscript inched and lurched forward; at every stage, she gave wise, informed, detailed, and challenging feedback. For all that I am very grateful. I have also enjoyed working with two other excellent editors—Brigitte Pelner and Linda Truilo—and I thank them for doing such a fine job of bringing my book through the publication process.

Ohio State's Melton Center for Jewish Studies supported my research with two travel fellowships. The College of Arts and Humanities helped by granting me a research sabbatical for 2008–2009. On the other hand, being around Ohio State had many benefits. I received much encouragement from Anna Grotans, as well as from Gregor Hens and Nina Berman, two colleagues who became dear friends long before we all wound up together at Ohio State, ten years ago. Furthermore, numerous other colleagues at the University deserve thanks for weighing in, in ways that mattered. They include Alan Beyerchen, Yossi Galron, Matt Goldish, Fritz Graf, Sarah Johnston, Robin Judd, Steve Kern, Bernhard Malkmus, Brian McHale, May Mergenthaler, Chris Otter, Jim Phelan, Brian Rotman, Maurice Stevens, Michael Swartz, Andrew Teitelbaum, and Jennifer Willging.

During the winter semester of 2010, I was a fellow at the Frankel Institute for Advanced Judaic Studies, at the University of Michigan; and in addition to enjoying my time there, I profited from it greatly. As everyone who has experienced it knows, the Institute is a wonderful, intellectually invigorating place. Talking about my work with Todd Endelman, the Institute's acting director and a perspicacious fellow traveler in the

Wissenschaft of Jewish self-hatred, proved especially rewarding. But there were many other fruitful discussions, some of which I had even before my fellowship began. In the fall of 2009, Scott Spector organized a symposium on Central European Jewish studies at the Frankel Institute, and in this context, I received valuable suggestions from key figures in the field, namely, Steve Aschheim, Leora Auslander, Mary Gluck, Scott Spector, Michael Steinberg, and Liliane Weissberg. Beyond all that, Nick Block, my research assistant at the Institute, was never less than stellar.

I feel very fortunate to have had the opportunity to present my work-in-progress in many impressive venues—the University of California, Davis, the University of Notre Dame, Duke University, Northwestern University, the University of Virginia, Reed College, and Leibnitz Universität in Hanover. In every case, exchanges with my hosts helped make my book better, and so I want to thank those hosts, among whom were Jaimey Fischer, Gail Finney, and Daniel Stolzenberg of UC Davis; Robert Norton of Notre Dame; Bill Donahue of Duke; Peter Fenves of Northwestern; Chad Wellmon, Völker Kaiser, and Jeffrey Grossman of UVA; Katja Garloff, Ben Lazier, and Ülker Gökberk of Reed; and Alexander Kosenina of Leibnitz Universität.

Staff members at Hanover's Stadtarchiv were extraordinarily affable and helpful. In Hanover, I also had the pleasure of meeting Rainer Marwedel, the author of a—or rather, *the*—biography of Theodor Lessing, and I am indebted to Dr. Marwedel for sharing with me his hard-won expertise. I am similarly indebted to Walter Schübler, who is working on what will be the definitive life of the other main character in *On the Origins of Jewish Self-Hatred*: Anton Kuh. With much wit and insight, Dr. Schübler answered more questions than I had any right to ask him.

Andy Markovits and Sam Moyn were just as generous. They read and incisively commented on parts of the manuscript, as did Noah Isenberg, who has been a close friend since we were in graduate school together at UC Berkeley, back in the 1990s. Brett Wheeler, another great friend from graduate school, read multiple drafts of chapters and endured endless trouble-shooting sessions. Without his heroic patience and remarkably astute input, this book would be very different—that is, much worse.

I thank my father, Robert Reitter, and my brother, Nicholas Reitter, for their interest in my work, as well as for being such agile, energetic, and supportive interlocutors. Maria Miller, too, listened to a lot of talk about the origins of "Jewish self-hatred," but that is really the least of what I owe her. This book is dedicated to Maria and our daughter, Cecelia.